FRONTIER NATION

HOW CANADA CAN BUILD A SUSTAINABLE ECONOMIC GATEWAY

RAVI NAIR

Frontier Nation: Building Canada's Next Century

First published in Canada in 2026 by
Ravi Nair

Mississauga, Ontario, Canada

ISBN 978-1-0674974-0-8 (Hardcover – Dust Jacket Edition)

ISBN 978-1-0674974-1-5 (Hardcover – Case Laminate Edition)

ISBN 978-1-0674974-2-2 (Paperback)

ISBN 978-1-0674974-3-9 (eBook)

Library and Archives Canada Cataloguing in Publication Data:

A catalogue record for this book is available from Library and Archives Canada.

Set in Garamond and Avenir typefaces.

Cover design: RS Creative Innovations

Copyedit: Dominic Farrell

PRAISE FOR *FRONTIER NATION*

"Frontier Nation makes a compelling and timely case for Global Gateway Zones as a powerful catalyst for national excellence and economic opportunity. With clarity and conviction, Ravi Nair aligns enduring Canadian values with the creation of bold, future-facing economic hubs, offering a visionary roadmap to attract global talent and secure prosperity for generations to come.

For leaders, policymakers, and thoughtful readers, this book is a rare study in how a nation can evolve without sacrificing its identity. It is a measured yet inspiring call to leadership—one that balances ambition with integrity, and innovation with principle.

Written with precision and accessibility, *Frontier Nation* is an engaging and rewarding read for policymakers, influencers, and general audiences alike."

— **Balakrishnan Kunnambath** CFA, Former Vice Chairman, Credit Suisse.

"At a time when Canada is confronting a changing global landscape and re-examining long-held assumptions, Ravi Nair offers constructive ideas for unlocking the country's potential. *Frontier Nation* is an ambitious and thoughtful effort that explores how economic growth can be made more innovative and inclusive - especially for Canadians who feel distant from decision-making and its benefits."

— **Joe Horneck**, Councillor, City of Mississauga, Ontario

"Frontier Nation confronts major problems that are paralyzing Canada with a serious case for moving from process gridlock to results. Ravi Nair's initiative and ingenuity make this worth consideration."

— **Peter Shurman**, Writer and Broadcaster

"A captivating must-read narrative non-fiction book, blending factual analysis, national policy strategy and literary storytelling to present a visionary roadmap for Canada's economic social and global transformation."

— **Dr. Madan Roy**, Professor Emeritus, McMaster University

"Frontier Nation strikes a much needed chord on what is paralyzing modern democracies. It offers a progressive but pragmatic solutions based roadmap to move away from process gridlock, providing an ambitious growth strategy grounded in real world challenges of trust, transitions and delivery."

— **Mike McQuaid**, Retired Senior Executive, UK Health and Social Care Sector

CONTENTS

EDITION STATEMENT

This edition of *Frontier Nation* is a narrative adaptation of the Canadian Frontier Development Zones (CFDZ) and Canada Global Gateway (CGGZ) policy blueprint, authored by Ravi Nair. A technical and institutional version (Policy Edition) is maintained for government, academic, and investor reference.

DISCLAIMER

This book is a work of visionary nonfiction. While based on documented policy research and public data, portions of the text incorporate dramatized dialogue and narrative elements to illustrate conceptual frameworks. All scenarios, characters, and conversations are fictionalized for narrative clarity. The views expressed are solely those of the author and do not represent any government or organization.

CONTACT

For speaking engagements, media inquiries, or research collaborations:
ravi@ravinair.net

"Ideas become history only when they are shared."

PREFACE

It began on a winter morning in Mississauga, the kind of morning when the air feels sharper than thought. The news ran yet another story about Canada's housing shortage. The anchor said, almost casually, that Canada — the second largest country on Earth — was running out of space.

That sentence stayed with me all day.

How could a nation with so much land and potential feel small? How could we be shrinking inward while the rest of the world was expanding outward?

That night, I sat at my desk and began sketching circles on a blank page — each one a city imagined from principle: powered by clean energy, connected digitally, open to the world. Not a dream, but a design.

The sketch that began as a restless thought on a cold Mississauga morning refused to fade. Something in that winter light made the country feel paused — as if the land itself were waiting for us to remember what it was capable of. It followed me through flights, conversations, and half-slept nights — a whisper reminding me that ideas belong not only on pages, but in places. In time, the whisper stopped being a thought and became a decision — in the most Canadian way possible: quietly, over coffee, beside a river still half-frozen.

That was where the story of *Frontier Nation* began — not as a plan, but as a promise: a country built on fairness could also build on purpose, and the space we have been blessed with might finally be matched by the courage to use it well.

PROLOGUE

THE QUIET COUNTRY

Snow fell softly over the Ottawa River, wrapping Parliament Hill in a quiet kind of dignity. The air was crisp, the sky a dim silver, and the city below seemed to move at half speed — calm, precise, unhurried. On mornings like this, Ottawa looked less like a capital and more like a promise: a place where order could become purpose, if someone simply decided to turn the key.

At a small table outside a Tim Hortons, two old friends sat in conversation. Steam rose from paper cups, curling into the November chill.

One of them was Evelyn Rousseau — a senior planner in the quiet machinery of Ottawa, known for turning government blueprints into something more human. The daughter of a Quebecois father and a Cree mother, she carried both histories without ceremony: the patience of policy and the precision of craft. Her notebooks, filled with tight lines of handwriting and loose sketches of cities, were part diary, part design. She believed that good government was not the absence of risk, but the art of measured courage. Evelyn had long been the quiet centre of complicated systems — someone who could hold policy and people in the same thought.

Across from her sat Arjun Mehta, recently returned after two decades abroad. He had lived in cities that forced themselves into being — Singapore, Dubai, Tel Aviv — places where ambition had been the only natural resource.

"It's funny," he said, his voice low. "Everywhere I worked, people spoke of Canada with respect. They call it fair and safe and decent. But never … daring."

Evelyn smiled faintly. "Maybe we've become the country that waits for others to lead — and then politely applauds."

Arjun nodded. "Comfort doesn't build the future." He paused, eyes flicking to the Peace Tower clock through the window. "I came back because I think Canada's story isn't finished. Maybe peace isn't the destination. Maybe it's the platform."

Outside, buses hummed through slush. A handful of public servants hurried past, collars up against the cold. The bell sounded the hour, a gentle insistence that time was still moving, even if the country felt content to let it pass.

Arjun glanced at Evelyn's notebook. "You ever feel like this city has been rehearsing for a performance no one will schedule?"

"All the time," she said, flipping to a page where she had roughed in a harbour district and a rail spur. "But rehearsals can end."

The idea that had lived quietly in Arjun's mind for years — first conceived far from home — seemed to find a voice in that moment. Not an invention of the morning, but a confirmation. What he had seen on three continents wasn't magic. It was design, discipline, and decision. If nations with almost nothing could build futures out of imagination, surely a nation with Canada's abundance could build out of intention.

Not in a boardroom. Not in a manifesto. Here, over coffee beside the Ottawa River, a quiet capital at the edge of winter, the belief finally felt like a plan.

Canada is admired for its fairness, its decency, its peace. It has never demanded the world's attention; it has earned the world's trust. That is no small inheritance. But admiration is not the same as ambition. The question before the country is no longer whether it can preserve what it has built; the question is whether it can renew it — turn civility into competitiveness, stability into strategy, and broad trust into real momentum.

The world offers lessons. Finland, small and cold, transformed itself through education and design. Estonia digitized government from the ground up and made bureaucracy almost invisible. Israel turned scarcity into innovation. South Korea made discipline a development model. The United Arab Emirates built investor confidence into infrastructure at scale. Each refused to let circumstance define destiny.

Canada's circumstance is different — not scarcity, but abundance. Oceans on two sides and an Arctic opening a third. Forests that breathe for the planet, freshwater that could quench continents, mineral wealth for the clean-energy age. A democratic culture of trust the world envies. What Canada lacks is urgency.

We regulate before we imagine. We consult before we construct. We confuse caution for wisdom. None of those instincts are wrong; they simply aren't enough anymore. If the twentieth century rewarded patience, the twenty-first rewards purpose.

The framework for that purpose has a name: Canadian Global Gateway Zones (CGGZ). The framework is not a rejection of Canadian character; it is its evolution. The idea is simple: a nation built on fairness can also lead with boldness — without abandoning either.

When I returned to Canada after years abroad, I was struck by its beauty — and its restraint. I had watched ports carved from sand, universities sprout among shipyards, and startup districts grow where warehouses once stood empty. In those places, ambition was an operating system. Here, progress moved at the pace of our winters: steady, polite, and slow.

This book is not a criticism of Canada. It is an act of faith in it. No other country is as prepared — politically, morally, institutionally — to show that capitalism can be clean, inclusive, and conscious. Canada doesn't need to become Singapore or Finland or Israel. It needs to become a more courageous version of itself, one that builds, invites, and leads without losing its decency. It must use its fairness not as an anchor, but as a launchpad.

The CGGZ program envisions a network of self-sustaining, co-governed economic cities across underutilized regions — from the Prairies to the Atlantic, from northern Ontario to gateways in the Yukon. Each city blends renewable energy, digital governance, and open pathways for skilled immigration to attract global talent and investment, while remaining firmly accountable to Canadian values.

Land leased, not sold — fifty to ninety-nine years — preserving national ownership and Indigenous stewardship while offering investors and institutions the certainty to build for the long term. Workforces with up to 80 percent skilled foreign specialists and at least 20 percent Canadian residents, ensuring knowledge transfer and upward mobility for local talent. Every decision — from tax rates to transit routes — is tracked on a real-time public platform that citizens and investors can see. Transparency isn't a press release; it's a public scoreboard. Not a once-a-year report, but a live, online dashboard where anyone can track approvals, timelines, hiring ratios, environmental indicators, and money in/money out.

These are not "special economic zones" in the old sense — no walled enclaves, no shortcuts for the connected. They are living laboratories for a new social contract: clean energy and water, fair governance, and an ambitious purpose. A model that says Canada can lead the world without ceasing to be itself.

A city built this way looks different. Its skyline feels like a promise made visible: timber mid-rises built for families, an energy plant that runs clean, a research hub beside the rail line — design choices that signal what the city values.

Wind towers and rooftop greenhouses, mid-rise timber housing warmed by district energy, a waterfront where research labs share a boardwalk with cafes and community markets. On the edge of town, a logistics yard hums beside a training campus where apprentices and Ph.D. students learn side by side. Freight moves at night to keep streets quiet by day. Public Wi-Fi is as common as crosswalks. The transit app and the tax code speak the same language.

It is not utopia. It is Canada, used on purpose.

At the entrance of the first Gateway council building, the Four Pillars would be etched into the stone: *Values. Discipline. Freedom. Stewardship.*

They are not slogans. They are cornerstones — the moral base of a nation that insists prosperity answer to principle.

- **Values:** Markets must serve moral purpose, not the other way around.
- **Discipline:** Vision without execution is performance art. Singapore taught the world that meritocracy, clear timelines, and clean governance turn smallness into strength. We don't imitate the city-state; we adopt its seriousness.
- **Freedom:** Liberty is not license. Diefenbaker's conviction — freedom carries responsibility — remains the Canadian centre of gravity. The point of Gateway Cities is not deregulation; it is regulation that is timely, transparent, and proportionate.
- **Stewardship:** The land is not commodity; it is relationship. Indigenous wisdom reminds us we belong to the land. Shared leases, co-governance, and conservation corridors turn reconciliation from rhetoric to rule.

We place those four words at the threshold so no one forgets what's important: ambition reports to ethics — not the reverse.

If you want to find the soul of this idea, don't start in Ottawa. Start in Thunder Bay in January, with the wind coming off Lake Superior like a lesson. Stand by the rail lines, half-buried in snow, and listen for what they used to carry: grain and ore and the stubborn belief that a country could knit itself together across snow and silence. Or go to Churchill, Manitoba, where the sky ripples green in winter and a rail line meets the bay like a promise, and ask whether a country so connected to oceans should be shy about trade. Then follow the old survey roads into northern Ontario, where abandoned airstrips glitter under moonlight. Listen to the empty hangars. They sound like unfinished sentences.

Frontier. The word still carries echoes of conquest, yet its root is simple: *frontière* — the line of meeting. The place where one world touches another. That is exactly what Gateway Cities intend to be: points of meeting between old industries and new ideas, between settlers' economies and Indigenous stewardship, between domestic workers and global migrants who choose to belong.

A frontier can divide or connect. Canada has the chance to make it connective.

The frontier isn't behind us. It's wherever courage begins again.

What would it mean to govern as if time were a public trust? It would mean approving in months what now takes years — without skipping the hard questions. It would mean measuring success in the open: approvals published with timestamps, environmental thresholds tracked like vital signs, housing completions counted in real time, public hearings streamed and archived. It would mean a civil service paid and promoted for outcomes — not optics. And it would mean a politic system that admits the truth: indecision is a decision, and delay is a tax — paid by those who can least afford it.

None of that requires Canada to become unrecognizable. It asks Canada to become fully itself: fair and firm, modest and modern, careful and quick. The world already trusts Canadian law and Canadian people. The Gateway experiment is simply a way to turn that trust into capacity — to build systems big enough to match our geography and growth.

Picture a young engineer from Chennai or Lagos or São Paulo unlocking an employment pass on arrival and walking straight into a lab that partners with a nearby plant. Picture a Red Seal carpenter from Windsor training twenty apprentices on a mass-timber housing site by the harbour. Picture a Dene entrepreneur winning a maintenance contract because procurement no longer treats "local" as a footnote. Picture a university satellite campus whose graduation ceremony happens in the same week as the launch of a new production line down the road.

Prosperity becomes a pattern. The city stops feeling like an exception and starts feeling like a prototype.

Evelyn closed her notebook and pushed her coffee cup aside. "We've spent a century proving we're good," she said. "Maybe the next one should prove we're great."

Arjun smiled. “Maybe greatness doesn’t mean louder. It just means braver.”

They stood. The snow had thickened outside, blurring the light along Wellington Street. The river below lay still under a skin of ice, but the air had changed — the charged quiet that comes just before something begins.

Arjun looked once more toward the Ottawa River and thought about the map in his head: rail spurs and research parks, long-lease neighbourhoods with playgrounds and workshops, a shipping schedule coordinated with night-freight to keep mornings for school buses and coffee lines. None of it outrageous. All of it obvious — if a country decided that its reputation for fairness could be matched by a reputation for getting things done.

This book is not a plan to make Canada into someplace else. It is a blueprint for finishing what Canada started: a nation that proves prosperity can be principled, velocity can be virtuous, and growth can be governed by the very values that made this country worth building in the first place. Somewhere between the bells and the snowfall, a quiet country began to wake.

When the snow finally melted along the Ottawa River, the idea that had been spoken in the hush of a Tim Hortons found wings. The questions that had hung in the air — Why not us? Why not now? — demanded geography. So, he packed a single notebook, a map marked with rail lines and river ports, and flew north. If Ottawa had been the conversation, Thunder Bay would be the test.

The stillness of Ottawa gives way to the vastness of the North.

PART I

THE RECKONING: SEEING CANADA CLEARLY

1

THE FRONTIER IDEA

The propeller plane banked gently over the edge of Lake Superior, its silver surface patterned with thin ribbons of ice. Below, an endless mosaic of pine, rock, and snow stretched to the horizon — a wilderness so vast it felt alive.

Arjun Mehta leaned against the window, watching the northern expanse unfold beneath him. He'd lived in places where necessity sharpened ambition — cities that treated planning like survival. Yet here, flying over Ontario's forgotten heartland, he felt a quiet paradox. Canada possessed everything those nations lacked — land, water, minerals, stability — and yet it hesitated to move.

"You could fit half of Europe down there," the pilot said through the intercom.

"And still have room for imagination," Arjun murmured, almost to himself.

When the plane landed in Thunder Bay, the wind rolled off the lake with a sharpness that made the air feel electric. The city was modest but weathered and awake — rail yards dusted with snow, the docks frozen still, the people grounded in a rhythm of endurance. It was Canada in miniature: calm, capable, and waiting.

In that moment, Thunder Bay felt like a frontier — not because it was lawless or remote, but because it sat at the edge of Canada's two realities: the crowded corridor to the south and the vast underused north beyond it. It was not a relic of the past, but a foundation for the future. The frontier was not a place to escape to — it was a place to begin again.

Since Europeans first arrived, Canada has told itself a story of movement — of rails, rivers, roads, and reinvention — people pushing through snow and silence to connect a continent. But somewhere along the way, the country stopped moving. It settled for a comfortable stasis — economically, imaginatively, and geographically.

Today, 90 percent of Canadians live within a day's drive of the U.S. border, crowded into cities that are vibrant but strained. Beyond them lies a different Canada — vast, rich, and quiet — a Canada that the rest of the world is scarcely aware of. Where other nations fight over land, Canada's land waits for its people.

The Frontier Idea is not about conquering or claiming. It is about *completion*. It imagines what it would mean to finally build out the potential of the country — responsibly, sustainably, and inclusively. It proposes a new compact between geography and governance, one that treats space not as emptiness to be preserved untouched, but as opportunity to be shaped with purpose.

This idea does not defy Canadian values; it fulfills them.

I've long believed land teaches what books can't: scale, humility, patience. In Singapore I saw how necessity breeds invention; in Dubai, how imagination can bend geography; in Finland and Israel, how constraint becomes discipline. Then I came home to Canada — abundant in land, peace, and talent — and noticed something unsettling: our abundance had bred hesitation. We've become fluent in balance, less fluent in boldness. The Frontier Idea grew from that paradox: a call to turn Canada's vastness into strategy, its peace into platform, and its fairness into forward motion.

The Frontier Idea is not about expanding borders; it is about expanding balance. The Frontier Idea imagines three simple but radical shifts.

1. **Redistribution of growth** — moving population and industry away from congested corridors toward underdeveloped regions in the Prairies, Atlantic Canada, and the North. These areas have the space and resources for a new kind of prosperity, one that is local, renewable, and sustainable.
2. **Reconstruction of industry** — rebuilding manufacturing, logistics, and clean energy hubs under a new model of Canadian Global Gateway Zones. These zones would not be enclaves of privilege or deregulation, but transparent, co-governed cities that operate as laboratories for innovation.
3. **Reconciliation through prosperity** — ensuring that Indigenous partnership is not symbolic but structural. Every Gateway Zone begins with consultation and ends with co-ownership. Because reconciliation is not just moral necessity — it is the smartest form of economics.

Each compact city would run on renewable energy managed by digital systems where every approval, exception, and expenditure leaves a trace — time-stamped, searchable, and visible to auditors and the public. They would invite foreign investors and skilled immigrants to co-build, but always on Canadian terms. These are not special economic zones; they are exemplars of an ethos — living demonstrations of what fair, clean, ambitious capitalism can look like.

There are many nations that turned limitation into leadership. Canada's challenge is the reverse: abundance that breeds inertia. We are patient, careful, and kind — virtues that have built peace but can also delay progress. Comfort is a beautiful thing, but it cannot be a legacy. The future punishes pauses.

If we continue to grow only where it is easy, we may one day realize we've mistaken comfort for progress — and delayed the building our future required.

The true challenge for Canada is not *where* we should grow, but *how we should grow well.* The Frontier Idea proposes replacing the old formula of extract-and-exit — whether the resource is timber, minerals, labour, or data — with build-and-belong investment that leaves skills, institutions, and long-term capacity behind. Partnership means building with Indigenous nations — not merely near them. Purpose means designing growth that serves humanity — not just markets. Prosperity means ensuring that the benefits of development ripple outward — not upward.

Every nation has a defining mission. For some, it is conquest. For others, defence. For Canada, it must be *dignity* — the ability to lead without arrogance and build without exploitation.

As Arjun stood by the frozen rail lines that cut across Thunder Bay that morning, the wind carried a whisper of iron and snow. The same tracks that once connected Canada's coasts now lay quiet, half-buried in snow. He imagined them one day alive again — carrying workers, materials, ideas — stretching deep into an awakened land.

"We've always had the map," he thought. "We just lacked the courage to follow it."

The sun broke through a gap in the clouds, casting a pale gold light over the frozen lake. In that moment, the horizon didn't look empty anymore. It looked ready. Thunder Bay made the question unavoidable: if a place this ready could wait so long, what did that say about the country's capacity to act?

Every frontier begins as a feeling and becomes a framework. On the flight back from Thunder Bay, Arjun began sketching grids over the wilderness below — not to conquer it, but to understand it. What if prosperity could be drawn like architecture? What if cities could be built to balance ambition with belonging? The idea was no longer abstract. It had coordinates, corridors, and a purpose bold enough to need proof.

The idea finds its first coordinates.

2

THE CASE FOR GATEWAY CITIES

Dawn spilled through a thin curtain of snow as the train rolled east out of Winnipeg. Frost feathered the windows; somewhere beyond the railyards, a line of birch trees flashed silver in the light. Arjun watched the city recede and felt again that familiar mixture of admiration and impatience. Canada's cities worked — too well, perhaps. They absorbed ambition the way a sponge absorbs water, leaving little to irrigate the rest of the land.

The car was nearly empty. A nurse on her way to Toronto scrolled headlines on her phone; a student napped beneath a hoodie; a farmer studied the weather radar. Each belonged to the country that Canada had become — urban, connected, compressed along a thin southern belt. Beyond that belt stretched a silence larger than most nations.

If the Prologue's conversation had been theory, this was its proof. The geography outside the train window explained everything: why the cost of housing had outpaced wages, why young workers clustered in four metropolitan regions, why rural schools closed even as cities ran out of classrooms. The country's engine idled in first gear.

Gateway Cities were the missing gears.

The idea sounds simple. Build where Canada has stopped building. In strategic corridors — near ports, rail spurs, or renewable-energy basins — establish new urban anchors designed from the ground up for twenty-first-century life. Compact, carbon-neutral, digitally governed. Places where manufacturing, research, and housing evolve together instead of colliding later.

But this simple vision demands complex execution. Every Gateway must meet three criteria: economic, ethical, ecological. Each must create jobs without draining neighbouring towns, invite immigration without inflaming inequality, and generate growth without damaging land or eroding trust. Canada's advantage is that it can afford to design this balance before crisis forces it.

The world has already run the experiment in fragments. South Korea's Incheon Free Economic Zone integrated logistics with universities and start-ups. Finland built the Oulu Innovation District around a single telecommunications hub. The United Arab Emirates turned Jebel Ali from desert into a trade port that now moves nine million containers a year. None of these places copied one another; they shared only one conviction — that geography should serve imagination.

For Canada, imagination begins with realism. Investors need clarity. Communities need continuity. And governments need courage to let both flourish at once. The mechanics mattered — leases long enough to attract capital, hiring models designed for knowledge transfer, and transparency built into the rules.

"Numbers prove need," Evelyn said quietly, "but a sense of belonging can't be measured in spreadsheets. If Gateway Cities forget that, they'll be efficient — and empty."

Arjun nodded, and for a moment the charts on the screen looked less like forecasts than like promises waiting to be kept.

Each zone would publish its data — tax revenue, hiring ratios, energy mix — on a live public dashboard. Transparency would replace slogans, creating a currency of trust.

Tax incentives would favour reinvestment over extraction: profits used to expand facilities would be taxed less than profits exported abroad. Municipal charters would tie executive bonuses to community metrics — school enrolment, air quality, apprenticeship numbers — so that growth meant more than quarterly gain.

In contrast to past free-economic zone experiments, success would not be measured only in economic terms it would include emotional criteria as well. Previous attempts to build special treated development as exceptional, peripheral, temporary. Gateway Cities treat it as ordinary, central, permanent. They are not special zones but *sample versions* of the country Canada wants to be.

Arjun had seen what happened when ambition outpaced conscience. He remembered the glass canyons of Dubai, dazzling and brittle, the workers' buses that left before dawn. He admired the achievement but also the absence — the missing idea of citizenship. Canada could do better precisely because it refused to look away from questions of fairness. Here, moral hesitation could become moral design.

He imagined a city on the northern shore of Lake Superior, its skyline a line of timber mid-rises warmed by district energy; a research park beside the rail terminal; streets quiet because freight moved at night. He imagined another near Halifax, feeding the Atlantic corridor with green hydrogen exports. And one in the Prairies: a logistics-education hybrid where drones shared airspace with grain elevators. None of it impossible; all of it inevitable once Canada decided to replace caution with competence.

That night, the blueprints followed him home — not on paper, but in thought.

The dining table was half-covered with sketches and printouts. Rhia, his daughter, leaned on her elbows, studying a crude map of northern Ontario. "You really think people will move there?" she asked.

Arjun smiled. "People moved to the Arctic for gold and to Mars for data. Why not here — for purpose?"

Anika, his wife, appeared from the kitchen doorway, wiping her hands on a towel. "And what about the people who already live there?" she asked gently.

"That's the point," Arjun said. "It only works if it starts with them."

Tintin, their little Shih Tzu, thumped his tail against the floor and barked once, as if approving the plan. Rhia laughed. "Looks like you've got your first supporter."

Anika placed a steaming bowl on the table. "Dreams need dinner before they need diagrams," she said, sliding into the chair beside him.

Arjun looked at the two of them — the patience in Anika's eyes, the curiosity in Rhia's — and realized that every plan worth building began at a kitchen table — not in a conference room. History suggests that renewal rarely begins at the centre. The national railway started as a frontier gamble. So did the oil sands, the Trans-Canada Highway, and universal healthcare. Each was dismissed as unrealistic until it simply existed. It sounds contradictory, but it's a Canadian pattern: we hesitate longer than we should — then move faster than anyone expects. The country's character has always combined patience with surprise.

The Gateway proposal carries that tradition forward but changes its compass: north instead of south, inclusive instead of extractive, clean instead of combustible. Where the last century's megaprojects traded wilderness for wealth, the next century must pair wisdom with endurance.

Every Gateway must therefore begin with partnership. Indigenous nations are not stakeholders; they are co-founders. The leases that underpin the zones must embed revenue sharing, land stewardship, and cultural preservation. Reconciliation can't remain ceremonial; it has to show up in contracts, revenue-sharing, and enforceable obligations.

The next afternoon, Arjun joined a policy roundtable by video, the screen divided between planners, engineers, and Evelyn's familiar face from Ottawa.

"Inclusion," she said, closing her notebook, "isn't sentiment — it's structure. If the contracts don't teach fairness, the laws never will. And if every project can show who benefits, we'll stop mistaking charity for partnership." Her tone carried the quiet authority of someone who had read too many equity reports that never left the office.

Second comes infrastructure. Roads, rails, and ports built once for extraction can be retrofitted for circulation — of goods, of data, of people. Canada's geography is not a burden; it is bandwidth.

Third is governance. Decision-making must compress. Permit times should be measured in months — not years. Environmental reviews must be digitized and public. Accountability needs to be made visible. Bureaucracy should behave like code: transparent, auditable, improvable.

Arjun continued, outlining how permits and accountability could be redesigned. Evelyn watched him sketch invisible systems in the air as he spoke. For years she had signed reports that measured efficiency by paperwork — not by outcome. *Maybe governance isn't slow,* she thought. *Maybe it's just afraid of being seen.* She smiled faintly. "Transparency isn't radical," she said. "It's overdue."

If those three principles sound technical, they are also moral. A government that moves slowly in the face of opportunity commits a quiet form of injustice — the denial of possibility.

At dinner that night in Toronto, Arjun met Evelyn again in a restaurant built inside a grand old post-office. The conversation turned from architecture to purpose.

"You're really going to call them Gateway Cities?" she asked.

"It fits," he said. "They aren't walls. They're doors."

She nodded, scribbling on the paper menu. "Every door needs a hinge. What's ours?"

He paused. "You've been circling it all along," he said. "Four values."

She looked up. "Say them."

He recited them quietly: Values. Discipline. Freedom. Stewardship. "Values," he explained, "because markets have to serve a moral purpose. Otherwise, efficiency becomes an end in itself — optimizing numbers while ignoring who benefits and who gets left out."

"Discipline," he continued, "because vision without follow-through is theatre. Lee Kuan Yew proved that discipline is the art of making tomorrow non-negotiable."

"Freedom," he said, "because Diefenbaker was right — liberty carries responsibility. Streamlining approvals doesn't mean abandoning standards; it means meeting them faster."

"And stewardship," he finished, "because the land isn't a resource; it's a relationship."

Evelyn smiled. "That's the geometry," she said. "Four points make a compass."

Outside, Toronto's towers glowed against the frozen harbour. Somewhere beyond those lights lay towns that once shipped steel, timber, wheat — towns now searching for the next opportunity to matter. Gateway Cities could be that opportunity. Not charity, not nostalgia — just relevance renewed.

The challenge is narrative as much as engineering. Canadians must learn to see frontier not as distance but as destiny.

At a small forum in Ottawa, Evelyn took the podium for the first time since the Gateway announcement. "Leadership," she told the room, "isn't the art of prediction — it's the art of permission: permission for a nation to surprise itself again. We've measured growth for a century. Now we must measure grace." The applause that followed was brief but sincere — the sound of recognition, not spectacle.

Arjun's train reached Montréal before dawn two days later. Snow flurries swept across the platform as he stepped onto the frozen concourse. He paused before the mural of early railway builders — a dozen faces chiselled in stone — and wondered what they would think if they could see the country now: wealthy, educated, safe, and yet waiting for permission to dream again.

He thought of the conversation in Ottawa, of the sketches in Evelyn's notebook, of the invisible map he carried in his head. A map where policy met poetry, where economics finally served ethics, and where the most Canadian quality of all — decency — was joined by its long-lost sibling, daring.

The first Gateway City, he decided, would not need fanfare. It would simply begin, as all Canadian revolutions begin — quietly and efficiently. And it would last forever.

As the northern lights shimmered above the river, Evelyn whispered the old Cree word for horizon — what the Cree language names so precisely — the line where land meets possibility.

But even the boldest idea must pass through humility. Before Canada could lead, it needed to listen. The world was already full of experiments

— some triumphant, some turbulent — that proved the physics of progress. On the train to Montréal, Arjun watched the snowy fields blur into motion and thought of other nations that had built not from wealth, but from will. To move forward, he would have to look outward.

Before Canada can design its own future, it listens to those who have built theirs.

3

LESSONS FROM THE WORLD

As the train pulled away from Montréal, Arjun thought of other nations that had faced their own crossroads — places where geography, scarcity, or circumstance had once seemed like permanent limits. Yet those same nations had reinvented themselves through design. They had treated development not as chance but as choice.

Canada, he realized, was not the first country to confront the paradox of potential without momentum. From Singapore's discipline to Chile's restraint, from Denmark's trust to Korea's ambition, the world had already run variants of the experiment Canada now debated. Each story carried its own method, its own moral. Together they formed a living trial — a set of parameters for how countries can move when they decide that survival is not enough.

Every nation tells itself a story about why it succeeds. Some attribute prosperity to geography, others to grit, still others to luck. But beneath every success story lies a simple truth: prosperity is designed. It rarely emerges from spontaneity; it is planned, cultivated, and governed into being.

Over the past half-century, countries with little in the way of land or resources have surpassed those blessed with both. Small states have learned to use limitations as spurs for ingenuity — transforming scarcity into efficiency, and constraint into inspiration. Singapore's industrial rise and Estonia's digital revolution show how nations with vision and discipline can rewrite the destiny of size.

For Canada, these examples are not blueprints to copy but success stories to study. They show what can happen when a government aligns ambition with execution, when public policy acts not as an obstacle but as a catalyst. They remind us that leadership can free a country from history or heritage through deliberate choices repeated over time.

The world's most successful development models share one quality: coherence. Their infrastructure, policy, and purpose align. They invent systems, destroy silos. Gateway Cities are not isolated projects but coordinated networks where investment, migration, and innovation reinforce one another.

SINGAPORE

Singapore's success is often spoken of as a miracle; in truth, it was the result of meticulous engineering. When independence arrived in 1965, the island had no natural resources, deep internal divisions, and an uncertain future. Its leaders, led by Lee Kuan Yew, responded not with ideology but with planning. Industrial estates replaced slums. Education became a national religion. Corruption was not tolerated; efficiency became a virtue. The Economic Development Board (EDB) served as a single-window agency — a concept later echoed in many free-zone regimes. It balanced foreign capital with domestic capacity, ensuring each foreign investment transferred skills and technology to Singaporeans. Over time, the nation evolved from an economy dominated by assembly lines to one of design labs, from one of factories to a centre of finance.

The city's greatest innovation, however, was its governance model: *a meritocracy that demanded results yet respected stability.* It proved that democracy's opposite is not efficiency, but indecision. Singapore showed that small nations can think big — provided they act quickly.

Prosperity begins with coherence. The Canada Global Gateway Zones must integrate policy, infrastructure, and human capital as one ecosystem — just as Singapore fused its ministries to foster a single national mission.

DUBAI

Dubai's ascent from desert outpost to global hub was not the result of luck; it was the product of logistics. Half a century ago, Dubai was a trading port with little more than ambition and sand. Today, it stands as one of the world's most connected cities, its skyline a tribute to what leadership and the embracing of risk can achieve in one generation. The emirate's formula combined *visionary governance* with *bureaucratic minimalism*. Where others debated regulations, Dubai built frameworks designed to send a simple message: *come, and build.* Its free-zone model — Jebel Ali Free Zone (JAFZA), Dubai Internet City, and Dubai International Financial Centre (DIFC) — turned real estate into a tool of economic diplomacy. By guaranteeing 100 percent foreign ownership, fast-track licensing, and building infrastructure that actually worked, Dubai transformed itself into a global hub for logistics, media, and fintech.

But beyond policy lay psychology. Dubai marketed optimism. It became the place where failure was permitted and speed rewarded — a sharp contrast to bureaucratic caution elsewhere.

Regulation can inspire as much as it restricts. CGGZ must re-imagine Canada's bureaucratic culture — replacing permission-based administration with outcome-based accountability, without compromising fairness or safety.

ESTONIA

Estonia regained independence in 1991 facing economic ruin and institutional vacuum. Lacking capital but rich in engineers, it made a radical decision: to rebuild as a digital-first nation. The result was the X-Road — a secure backbone connecting every government agency, business, and citizen. Taxes, health records, land titles, even voting became digital and transparent. In 2014, Estonia extended this infrastructure beyond its borders through e-Residency, allowing anyone in the world to register a business online under Estonian law. This simple innovation turned a nation of 1.3 million into a platform for millions more.

Digital governance reduced corruption, accelerated entrepreneurship, and slashed administrative costs. More profoundly, it redefined citizenship itself — from a birthright to a networked relationship.

Digital governance is not just modernization; it's sovereignty in the twenty-first century — because the rules live in systems now: identity, permits, benefits, procurement, enforcement. If those systems are slow, opaque, or outsourced, a government's authority becomes theoretical. If the CGGZ model embeds an open, secure data infrastructure — with transparent application programming interfaces (APIs) and shared access — Canada could become the most trusted destination for global digital enterprise.

ISRAEL

Israel's journey from desert to digital powerhouse began with necessity. Its transformation from a fragile state to a high-tech powerhouse defied its geography. With limited natural resources and constant security threats, it learned to innovate out of necessity. In the 1990s, the Yozma Program seeded Israel's venture-capital ecosystem by matching private funds with government equity. Military research was commercialized into civilian technologies; risk-taking became a national instinct. Israel's universities, defence sector, and private investors formed an "innovation triangle," where failure was considered a learning opportunity — not defeat. Start-ups born in Tel Aviv and Haifa went on to shape global cybersecurity, agritech, and medical-device markets.

Money wasn't the basis for its success; it was mindset — a cultural permission to question authority and experiment relentlessly.

Innovation cannot be taught; it must be enabled. CGGZ must nurture venture capital, academic research, and industry partnerships within the same ecosystem — and create an environment where calculated risk is celebrated — not penalized.

IRELAND

Ireland's renaissance began in the 1980s, when it decided that education was its only export. It was an economy of emigration, unemployment, and fiscal fragility. Its turning point came not from a reduction in tax rates alone, but from a quiet revolution in education and openness. The Industrial Development Authority (IDA) pursued a single principle: every investor must create knowledge — not dependency. Global technology and pharmaceutical firms were offered stable taxation and access to a well-trained, English-speaking workforce. By the late 1990s, Dublin's new skyline symbolized a nation that had traded low expectations for high skill.

Ireland's success was built on consistency: a low, predictable tax rate was part of the formula, but the deeper secret was stability. The 12 percent corporate tax rate remained unchanged for decades — the proof of a government that kept its word. Its universities aligned curricula with enterprise; its government spoke the language of predictability. Within two decades, Ireland turned emigration into immigration.

Tax incentives matter less than trust in policy. If CGGZ guarantees long-term clarity on taxation and talent mobility, investors will plan for generations — not election cycles.

RWANDA

Rwanda faced annihilation after the 1994 genocide. Few stories illustrate its institutional rebirth. After 1994, the country faced ruin: no infrastructure, no capital, and a devastated social fabric. Within two decades, it became one of Africa's most transparently and efficiently governed nations. Through disciplined planning, Rwanda digitized land titles, simplified business registration, and prioritized women in leadership. Its capital, Kigali, is now recognized as one of Africa's cleanest and safest cities. The Kigali Innovation City integrates education, information and communications technology (ICT), and entrepreneurship — proof that development can be designed around integrity.

Good governance multiplies every other investment. Transparency, accountability, and speed of delivery are not moral luxuries; they are competitive assets. For CGGZ, creating zones free from bureaucratic drag is a precondition for credibility.

CHILE

Chile has learned to treat prosperity as something to be managed — not consumed. Its path to prosperity is a study in steadiness. A nation vulnerable to earthquakes and commodity cycles decided to build its future on fiscal rules — not political whims. In 2006, it codified a structural budget surplus rule, saving copper-export windfalls in a sovereign wealth fund. When markets fell, the fund allowed the government to cushion citizens from the cost of public spending; when prices rose, it was used to curb inflation. Chile combined this discipline with steady liberalization and social investment. Its long-term contracts and investor-protection laws turned resource wealth into stability rather than temptation.

Resource abundance can serve sustainability if paired with restraint. CGGZ fiscal frameworks should emulate Chile's rule-based approach — balancing innovation incentives with intergenerational prudence.

ICELAND

Iceland's banking system imploded in 2008; its GDP shrank by 10 percent in a single year. The country responded not with denial but with redesign. It nationalized failed banks, restructured household debt, and recommitted to renewable energy as its industrial backbone. Within five years, growth had returned and confidence followed. Today, Iceland runs almost entirely on geothermal and hydro power. Its lesson is not about size, but self-correction: acknowledging error, acting fast, and investing in resilience.

Policy failure is not fatal when learning is institutionalized. Each Gateway City must function like Iceland's energy model — able to recalibrate quickly when shocks arise. Adaptive governance is a sign of strength — not instability.

What unites these four nations is not geography, ideology, or scale. It is discipline after difficulty. They built confidence where there was crisis, continuity where there was uncertainty. Their leaders understood that credibility itself is infrastructure — every bit as vital as roads or power grids.

For Canada, these examples are reminders that reform need not wait for collapse. Change can be anticipatory — not reactive. The CGGZ vision should embody that mindset: a pre-emptive reinvention before stagnation hardens into decline.

CHINA

China's modern rise began as an experiment. Few transformations in human history match China's. When Deng Xiaoping opened the nation's economy in 1978, he did not issue a single plan but, instead, invited a thousand local experiments. The Special Economic Zones (SEZs) — Shenzhen, Zhuhai, Shantou, and Xiamen — were pilot projects in limited capitalism. They offered clear land policy, tax incentives, and bureaucratic autonomy. If a policy worked, it was scaled; if not, it quietly disappeared. Shenzhen began as a fishing village of thirty thousand people; four decades later, it is a metropolis of over seventeen million and the hardware capital of the world. The pattern repeated nationwide: reform first, codify later. Behind that flexibility lay consistency — a long-term commitment to infrastructure, export orientation, and manufacturing excellence. Over forty years, China lifted hundreds of millions from poverty by making iteration a principle of governance.

Innovation flourishes when government treats regulation as iteration — not decree. The CGGZ framework should mirror China's experimental approach within a democratic context: start small, measure honestly, and scale only what proves to work. Policy pilots are not weakness; they are modern governance.

SOUTH KOREA

South Korea's "Miracle on the Han River" turned a war-torn agrarian society into a G7-class technology leader within two generations. The key was state-guided capitalism — a compact between government, finance, and industry. Through five-year economic plans, Korea directed credit toward export-oriented conglomerates (*chaebols*), built ports and shipyards ahead of demand, and embedded engineers inside ministries. Education became the great equalizer: by the 1990s, Korean high-school completion rates exceeded those of most OECD countries. When the Asian financial crisis struck in 1997, Korea again adapted — restructuring its debt, liberalizing capital markets, and doubling down on R&D. Today, Samsung, Hyundai, and LG are not just brands; they are symbols of a nation that viewed industrial competence as national identity.

Industrial coordination need not involve central control. The CGGZ model can borrow Korea's coherence while keeping Canada's pluralism, linking universities, financiers, and manufacturers into shared missions such as clean technology, advanced materials, and renewable energy systems.

China and Korea have different ideologies but shared one habit: they built before certainty. Each treated industrial growth as architecture, something to be drawn, engineered, and revised — not merely theorized. Their governments were not the builders of everything, but the designers of direction.

For Canada, this means recapturing ambition without abandoning accountability.

A modern democracy can coordinate industry through transparency instead of decree, through data instead of dogma. The Gateway Cities must become laboratories for that principle — where government sets the compass, markets power the engine, and citizens remain the owners of purpose.

DENMARK

Denmark offers a quiet, enduring model of prosperity — not driven by scale, but by *balance*. Its secret lies in "flexicurity" — the fusion of flexibility for businesses and security for workers. Employers can hire and adapt quickly; workers who lose jobs receive strong social support and rapid retraining. The result: an economy that moves fast without leaving people behind. Urban design follows the same philosophy. Copenhagen's city planners treat sustainability as an essential feature of infrastructure — not ornament. Cycling lanes, clean energy grids, and communal public spaces form a physical language of equality. Innovation, in Denmark's context, isn't only about technology — it's about *trust*. That trust enables efficient governance and consistent social contracts between citizens and state.

Growth that forgets people is decay. As Gateway Cities rise, they must integrate affordable housing, cultural access, and public well-being into their metrics of success. A frontier that excludes compassion is not progress; it's replication of old mistakes.

INDIGENOUS CANADA

Indigenous Canada: Before the first road or railway, Canada's land was governed through relationships — not ownership. Indigenous systems of stewardship treated territory not as property but as responsibility. Decisions about land use were made through councils, consensus, and continuity — a collective contract between generations. Modern policy often overlooks this depth, reducing inclusion to consultation. Yet, embedded within Indigenous governance are principles that align perfectly with the values Canada seeks to build: sustainability, accountability, and shared prosperity.

The Seven Grandfather Teachings — wisdom, love, respect, bravery, honesty, humility, and truth — mirror the moral geometry needed for economic renewal. These are not ceremonial virtues; they are governance tools. When adapted into modern frameworks like CGGZ, they can ensure that new growth honours both *people and place.*

Sustainability is not imported innovation; it is a rediscovered inheritance. Indigenous partnership is not symbolic — it's structural. The new frontier must be co-owned in spirit — not merely co-managed on paper.

Denmark and Indigenous Canada remind us that human dignity is the truest measure of progress. Taken together, these lessons form a simple equation: Growth = Leadership × Integrity × Design.

For Canada, this means embracing the paradox of being both old and young — a mature nation that must rediscover its frontier spirit. Our challenge is not capacity but conviction. We already possess land, education, energy, and diversity. What we need is coordination — the courage to connect vision with execution.

Frontier Nation proposes the Canada Global Gateway Zones as that connecting tissue — a policy architecture built from the best of the world, rooted in Canadian values.

In the chapters ahead, this framework moves from idea to implementation, from inspiration to institution. Where others built for survival, Canada can now build for purpose. The world has shown us how. It is time to make it our own.

Every lesson invites a response. Canada has studied the world's blueprints; now comes the harder part: answering the question of who will have the courage to draw its own blueprint. History remembers not only the nations that learned but those that led. Arjun knew that policies could be borrowed, but purpose had to be written from within. The next chapter of the journey would not be about examples — it would be about leadership.

Lessons mean little without leaders to live them.

PART II

THE DESIGN: BUILDING CITIES WORTHY OF THE FUTURE

4

THE LEADERSHIP IMPERATIVE

The snow had stopped by the time Arjun reached Ottawa. The city seemed wrapped in its own deliberations — cautious progress, committees waiting for consensus. He walked along the frozen canal toward Parliament Hill, past statues of men who had once imagined railways across emptiness and provinces stitched from courage. They had built their century out of conviction — not convenience. Now, a new century waited for someone to do the same. Leadership, Arjun thought, is not the act of commanding; it is the art of convincing a nation to believe again. Canada has never lacked intelligence or integrity; what it lacks, sometimes, is ignition.

The success of the Gateway idea would depend less on architecture than on attitude. The world's great transformations — Singapore's rise, Korea's reconstruction, even Canada's own Confederation — had not begun with plans. They had begun with permission: permission to try something extraordinary before it was universally approved.

A nation does not renew itself by waiting for unanimity.

Modern leadership in Canada often confuses caution with prudence. Policies are tested for optics before outcomes; ambition is rationed to avoid criticism. But a society cannot innovate if it treats disagreement as danger. The country's greatest achievements — the transcontinental railway, the Charter, Medicare — were not perfect at birth; they were perfected through courage. Leadership, in this sense, involves a moral choice. To move when the safe option is stillness. To decide before the data is complete. To listen without surrendering to inertia. In an age of algorithms and risk models, genuine leadership is human precisely because it cannot be automated.

Arjun had spent years studying how complexity becomes a shield — protecting delay, protecting vested interests, and protecting decisions from scrutiny. In every ministry he'd worked with, he saw good ideas die of over-analysis. Committees designed to ensure fairness became barriers to it. Too often in Canada, process becomes the product — a system calibrated to avoid mistakes rather than to create results. The more Canada tried to guarantee consensus, the less it achieved.

He imagined a new kind of leader: not the loudest in the room, but the clearest. One who could say, "This is what we're building, and this is why," and make that statement feel inevitable rather than radical. Every great reformer, from Roosevelt to Lee Kuan Yew, shared that gift. They spoke in sentences the public could finish for them. They made policy legible — so ordinary citizens could claim ownership of it. Canada's next transformation will require leaders fluent not just in economics but also in empathy. Clarity is not simplification of thought; it is compassion for the listener.

The twentieth century built bureaucracies to manage risk. The twenty-first must build stewardship to manage renewal. Stewardship is not administration; it is authorship. It recognizes that institutions are not machines but living systems that evolve with trust.

Arjun often thought about Evelyn's four words: Values. Discipline. Freedom. Stewardship. They weren't slogans; they were instructions for leadership.

- **Values** to ensure that ambition remains anchored in ethics.
- **Discipline** to convert vision into execution.

- **Freedom** to let new voices lead.
- **Stewardship** to remember that power is borrowed — not owned.

These are not merely personal virtues; they are the building blocks of credible government. Canada's leaders, at every level, will have to reclaim the old art of saying yes. Yes to complexity that can be solved. Yes to risk that can be managed. Yes to people who believe they belong in the story.

Leadership is also design. The way a nation organizes its decisions determines how fast it can dream. Countries like Denmark thrive because their institutions act as amplifiers, not mufflers, of purpose. Their bureaucracies execute policy at the speed a high-trust society should be able to move — fast, transparent, and accountable. Canada's federal model — broad, cautious, decentralized — has served peace well but progress poorly. To move from management to momentum, it needs a new structure of coordination: An agile centre capable of piloting change. Provinces empowered to localize it. Indigenous partners co-governing it.

The Gateway project offers exactly that strategy. It is not an alternative to Canada's system; it is a prototype for its evolution. If leadership can align federal vision, provincial execution, and Indigenous stewardship, then governance itself becomes a demonstration of democracy that works.

When Arjun spoke later that night to a small group of young policymakers at a cafe near Sparks Street, he said something that surprised even himself. "The failure of leadership is not absence of will," he told them. "It's the belief that the next generation will fix what this one postpones." He looked around at their faces — earnest, impatient, idealistic — and saw in them the same paradox that defined Canada: decency without daring.

"We have everything," he continued, "but we wait for permission to use it. That's not humility. That's hesitation disguised as virtue."

One of the students asked if he really believed Gateway Cities could change the country. "They won't change it," he said. "They'll remind it."

The silence that followed wasn't doubt — it was recognition. Leadership, Arjun realized, is not about command; it is about contagion. The courage of one leader can awaken the competence of a nation.

The train journeys, the sketches, the conversations — all of them pointed to one truth: Canada is ready. Ready for leaders who measure success not in polling numbers but in permanence. Ready for citizens who expect more than management. Ready for a politics that rebuilds instead of rebrands.

The next chapter of Canada's story will not be written in marble or mandates. It will be written in motion — in the roads and grids and classrooms of the first Gateway City, wherever it arises. Arjun thought again of Evelyn's words: "Every door needs a hinge." He smiled. Leadership is that hinge. The door can no longer wait to open.

Leadership, he realized, was not simply about vision. It was about promoting values that could survive contact with reality. And so, in the weeks that followed, the speeches and sketches began to harden into something measurable — a framework where ethics would sit not in footnotes but in budgets. If leadership is the compass, then the economy is the terrain. And it was time to map both.

Governance gains its compass.

5

A VALUES-BASED ECONOMY

The room smelled faintly of cedar and coffee. A small audience had gathered inside the lecture theatre of the University of Ottawa's Centre on Public Policy and Management — students, civil servants, and a handful of business leaders drawn by curiosity more than conviction. The evening's topic, *Markets and Morals in the Age of Transition,* sounded abstract until the first slide appeared behind the podium: "What is wealth for?"

Evelyn stood at the side wall, notebook in hand. Onstage, Arjun adjusted the microphone. "Every society," he began, "decides not only how to make money, but how to make meaning. The two decisions are supposed to be the same. Somewhere along the way, we let them drift apart."

The slide changed: a photo of a cargo ship gliding through the St. Lawrence, its containers stacked like coloured bricks against the grey sky.

"We measure GDP," he said, "but not the dignity that produced it — whether people can afford a home, raise a family, and feel secure. We count growth, but not the social stability that makes growth sustainable. When value is detached from values, we get clever policy that looks efficient on paper — and corrosive in real life."

He paused long enough for the silence to settle. "That's the real deficit we face — not fiscal, but moral."

Afterward, they walked out into the chill of Laurier Avenue. Snow brushed the hoods of passing cars; the canal lay frozen beneath the streetlights. Evelyn exhaled a white plume. "You made a few bureaucrats nervous," she said.

Arjun smiled. "That's usually a good sign."

They turned toward Confederation Square. The conversation drifted between theory and practice, between the words on the slide and the world outside. Canada, Evelyn said, had every advantage: stability, resources, education, civility. But, she noted, advantage without intention was inertia. The task now was to reconnect what a certain model of prosperity had pulled apart — community and mobility, growth and fairness, speed and trust.

Canada had always aspired to goodness. That was its strength and its trap. From the Charter of Rights and Freedoms to universal health care, the country had built fairness into its infrastructure. Yet fairness alone could not fund the future. Kindness had to learn efficiency; conscience had to learn courage.

A values-based economy is not one that preaches. It measures. It designs ethics into its operations the way engineers design safety into bridges. In such an economy, transparency replaces charity as proof of integrity. Investment follows governance — not rhetoric.

Economists and policymakers alike have argued that prosperity must rest on moral purpose — that markets exist to serve people — not the other way around. The line had echoed across boardrooms but rarely reached budgets. *Frontier Nation* sought to turn that sentence into scaffolding.

Every Gateway City, Arjun believed, would be a working example of that alignment. Renewable energy as default — not decoration. Tax codes rewarding reinvestment and training. Public dashboards showing emissions alongside employment. Ethics as architecture — not afterthought.

The next week, he flew to Calgary for meetings with industry groups. From the plane, he watched the Rockies tilt into view, black stone dusted white. On the horizon lay oilfields, wind farms, and a debate older than most careers: growth versus responsibility. He thought of Lee Kuan Yew's blunt observation: "I have always thought that a method that works is better than a theory that sounds good." The challenge for Canada was to make responsibility work.

The Calgary forum was cordial, skeptical, and exactly what he expected. Executives wanted certainty; community leaders wanted safeguards. "If we go green too fast, we lose competitiveness," one oilman argued. "If we go slow," a mayor replied, "we lose credibility." The tension was real and useful. Progress lived in that tension — not beyond it.

That evening, as the city lights shimmered on the Bow River, Arjun named the four pillars again — Values, Discipline, Freedom, Stewardship — not as slogans, but as tests. Each was meant to keep growth fast and fair, ambitious and grounded.

Back in Ottawa, Evelyn met him at the riverside walkway below Parliament. Ice cracked softly along the edges where meltwater seeped beneath the crust. "You think people will buy into a moral framework?" she asked.

"They already live by one," he said. "They just forgot to name it."

He explained how the pillars could translate into policy: Values embedded through open budgeting and equity audits; Discipline through performance-based civil service; Freedom through streamlined yet transparent approvals; Stewardship through long leases and renewable quotas. The architecture of ethics was also the architecture of efficiency.

Evelyn flipped through her sketchbook, where she had drawn a diagram of a city shaped like a compass. North was Stewardship, south was Values, east Discipline, west Freedom. At the centre she had written one word: *Trust.*

"That's what everything hinges on," she said. "If people stop trusting that the system is fair, none of it holds."

"Then we rebuild trust by letting them see how fairness works," he replied. "Not speeches. Dashboards."

In March, the first pilot site was announced: a manufacturing-research corridor near Sudbury. The news drew predictable questions: Could it compete with Toronto? Was it another subsidy scheme? Wasn't it too far north? Too cold? Yet within weeks, applications arrived from companies in Finland,

Japan, and India. They were drawn not only by incentives but by the rules themselves: clear, predictable, enforceable. Canada's moral reputation had become an economic asset.

By design, the pilot required at least one Indigenous majority-owned enterprise in each sector. The lease structure allocated 5 percent of revenue to local education and conservation. None of this was charity. When inclusion and environment are built into cost, risk falls and stability rises. Investors understand stability.

The announcement also triggered a wave of student interest. Universities proposed joint programs in sustainable logistics and ethical engineering. The country that once exported raw materials now exported governance models.

Economic historians often describe capitalism as a river — adaptive, unstoppable, occasionally destructive. But rivers can be guided. The new model didn't dam the flow; it carved channels where current meets conscience. Taxes that reward retention over repatriation. Credit linked to verified sustainability scores. Public procurement indexed to local training ratios. The invisible hand still moves; it simply carries a compass.

This, Arjun realized, was how Canada could outcompete larger powers: not by offering cheaper labour or deeper pockets, but by earning higher trust. In an age of volatility, trust is the new currency. Investors and immigrants alike choose it instinctively. The world already believes Canada is honest; Gateway Cities would prove that honesty scales. When information is public, integrity becomes contagious. Transparency doesn't just inform; it disciplines.

That summer, he travelled north again, this time to meet community leaders along James Bay. The plane dipped low over wetlands glittering like mirrors. Below lay villages accessible only by ice road or airstrip. The meeting hall smelled of coffee and spruce logs. Elders spoke first, describing both hope and hesitation. They had seen programs arrive with fanfare and depart with excuses. Why should this be different?

"Because you'll own it," Arjun said simply. "We lease the land together. You set the thresholds. We publish the results. No secrets, no second layer of signatures."

An elder nodded slowly. "Then start small," he said. "Show us the harvest before you plant another field."

Outside, children skated on a rink cleared from the snowpack. Arjun watched them weave between orange pylons and thought how every nation begins the same way — by balancing joy and risk on thin ice until the surface holds.

In Toronto that fall, the Values Forum convened economists, Indigenous entrepreneurs, and civic designers. The keynote panel was called "Ethics as Infrastructure." The phrase sounded academic until the speakers explained it: ethical design reduces friction the way good engineering reduces drag. A transparent permit process cuts cost like a better turbine cuts fuel. Morality, it turned out, was measurable.

One presenter cited Estonia's digital audit system, where citizens can see who accessed their records. Another showed how Norway's sovereign wealth fund publishes every investment's carbon impact. A third described Israel's innovation authority, which only funds start-ups that share patents with public universities. Canada's experiment, they agreed, could integrate all three — transparency, accountability, reciprocity — under one flag.

Evelyn's closing remark drew a standing ovation: "Ethics is not a constraint. It's Canada's competitive edge."

By winter, the snow had returned to Ottawa, heavier this time. The frozen river's surface was clean and unbroken, reflecting the pale lights of the city. In a small cafe — another Tim Hortons, another morning — Evelyn reread the draft of the *Frontier Nation* proposal while Arjun watched commuters queue for coffee.

"Do you ever worry it's too idealistic?" she asked.

He smiled. "Idealism built the railway, the Charter, and Medicare. The problem isn't idealism; it's forgetting to deliver."

He folded the pages, slid them into a folder and tapped the cover lightly. "If we can prove that values and velocity belong in the same sentence, we'll have done something bigger than draft another policy. We'll have written a manual for belief."

Evelyn looked toward the river. Snowflakes fell thick and slow, erasing footprints almost as soon as they formed. "Belief," she said, "and follow-through."

That evening, the wind rose across the valley, scattering the last leaves from Parliament Hill. The lights in the Peace Tower flickered against the sky, steady despite the gusts. Somewhere inside, long after the corridors emptied, a security guard on rounds paused before the marble tablet listing the country's founders and thought not of their politics but of their nerve — the audacity to imagine a federation where none existed, connecting provinces by promise and steel.

A century later, the task was not so different. The tools had changed; the spirit had not.

The frontier had moved — from land to law, from rails to values. The next act of nation-building would be written not in miles of track but in metrics of trust.

And when history looks back, it will not ask whether Canada had resources. It will ask whether it had resolve. Words, however noble, could not stay on whiteboards forever. Every reform, every revolution, needs a place to land.

By early spring, the sketches on Evelyn's desk had become site plans; the debate about values had turned into zoning maps and lease terms. Somewhere between theory and terrain, the first Gateway was about to rise — not as a symbol, but as a signal.

Years later, as the first Gateway City matured into proof rather than promise, Arjun found himself back where every idea begins: at the dinner table. The house in Mississauga felt familiar, though time had softened its edges. Framed sketches of the original Gateway blueprint lined the wall. Outside, the maple trees shimmered gold in the early fall light. Tintin dozed on his chair near the window, his paws twitching at dreams only dogs understand. Rhia sat across from her father, scrolling through photos on her tablet — sleek timber towers, wind corridors, a market square alive with music and trade. "They're calling it *Gateway City North* now," she said proudly.

Arjun smiled. "Good. It means it no longer needs my name."

Anika poured tea into mismatched mugs. "Hard to believe all this started with napkin sketches and cold coffee," she said.

He laughed softly. "And patience I didn't deserve."

Rhia looked up. "When you first told people your idea, they said it was impossible."

He nodded. "That's how I knew it mattered."

Tintin lifted his head, gave a small huff, and settled back to sleep. Outside, a light wind moved through the trees, its flow like the one that had carried an idea from a notebook to a nation. Arjun looked at Rhia and Anika, the future and the foundation sitting across from him. "You know," he said, "it was never really about building cities."

"What was it about, then?" Rhia asked.

He paused. "About proving that belief can be built in brick and glass."

The silence that followed was comfortable, full of completion. The kind that doesn't end a story — only rounds it.

Values demand verification.

6

THE BLUEPRINT OF TRUST

The morning air in Sudbury carried a mineral tang — steel, snow, and the faint sweetness of pine. Survey stakes dotted a cleared plateau south of the ring road, each topped with a strip of orange tape that fluttered like small flags of intention. Excavators rested beside portable offices where blueprints were taped to plywood walls. The site looked ordinary to anyone passing by, yet it was not. It was the first line of Canada's next paragraph.

Evelyn ran a gloved hand along the survey table, tracing the grid. "So, this is where the council chamber goes," she said.

Arjun nodded. "And over here, the transparency hub — the public data centre. Every permit, every environmental metric, live on screen."

She smiled. "A city that publishes its own conscience."

"That's the idea," he said. "Trust by design — not declaration."

Trust is rarely planned; it is usually inherited or eroded. Nations spend decades building it and moments losing it. Canada's fortune is that its institutions still command belief. The challenge is to convert that belief from static goodwill into dynamic infrastructure. In Gateway Cities, trust would not be sentimental. It would be systemic — embedded in law, layout, and code.

Each new city begins with a Charter of Transparency: a digital constitution written in plain language and visible to every resident. It lists what information must be public, what timelines are mandatory, and how citizens can challenge decisions. The charter functions like open-source software — inspectable, improvable, collectively owned. Bureaucracy becomes architecture: predictable, legible, secure.

The first principle of the blueprint is open data, closed corruption. Every Gateway project runs a mirror website that shows its heartbeat — budget flows, emissions, employment ratios, audit flags. The dashboard is not propaganda; it is performance. Instead of glossy reports, the public gets graphs that refresh by the minute. A citizen can watch a wastewater plant's output the way others track weather.

The second principle is shared oversight. Each zone's governing council includes municipal officials, Indigenous representatives, and two citizen jurors chosen by lot every year. Their meetings are streamed and archived. Votes are timestamped. Silence costs more than speech.

The third is reciprocal accountability. If a company receives incentives, its milestones are public; if the government delays approvals, the delay is logged. Trust becomes transactional in the healthiest way — recorded, auditable, mutual.

One afternoon a contractor asked Arjun, half-joking, if this level of transparency wouldn't scare investors. "Only the wrong ones," he answered. The right kind of capital doesn't flee sunlight; it demands it. The world's most successful markets — from Helsinki to Wellington — compete not on secrecy but on standards. Canada's export could be credibility itself.

He remembered a meeting in Singapore years earlier, when a minister told him, "Efficiency is just trust accelerated." The phrase had stayed with him. Now, in northern Ontario, it had become a blueprint: approvals issued within ninety days or automatically escalated; procurement open to any firm that meets published criteria; environmental data uploaded before shovels hit ground. No favours, no back doors, no mystery.

In the site canteen, workers compared notes over lunch. The foreman, a Métis welder from Thunder Bay, pointed at the QR code printed on the wall poster. "That's the portal," he said proudly. "You scan it, you see everything — how many locals hired, hours logged, even recycling rates. My kid checks it for her school project."

That, Arjun thought, was the measure of success: not a press release, but a schoolchild reading civic data as casually as weather. A culture that learns integrity by habit — not lecture.

Trust also needs rhythm. Every Gateway City operates on a Civic Calendar — quarterly public audits, biannual citizen assemblies, an annual *Festival of Progress* where residents review results before the next year's budget. Celebration becomes scrutiny, and scrutiny becomes tradition. In time, the calendar itself teaches that oversight is patriotic.

To prevent the old disease of red tape, the system adopts a paradox: the faster you publish, the slower you can cheat. Speed and honesty align. Digital signatures, smart contracts, and traceable workflows replace paperwork. Bureaucracy doesn't vanish; it performs better.

When construction paused for spring thaw, Arjun visited Ottawa to brief Parliament's Standing Committee on Regional Development. The room smelled of paper and politics. A veteran MP asked the question that lingered over every reform: "Why should Canadians believe this won't become another bureaucracy?"

Arjun answered, "Because everyone can watch it breathe." He described the dashboard, the juror system, the auto-escalation of permits. "It's bureaucracy with a mirror. When people can see the process, they stop assuming conspiracy."

Another member asked about cost. "Transparency pays for itself," he replied. "Fraud is expensive. Distrust is inflation."

The committee minutes later recorded unanimous support "in principle." In a country known for moderation, that was revolution enough.

Evelyn spent those weeks refining the city's civic spaces. She believed design could express ethics. The council chamber was circular, glass-roofed, oriented to the rising sun. The plaza outside doubled as farmers' market and protest ground — planned dissent built into the blueprint. "If citizens can't gather," she told the architects, "then it isn't democracy; it's décor."

Street lighting used sensors linked to energy dashboards. Buses were autonomous but free. Every building met zero-carbon codes; some produced more power than they consumed. The first school opened its doors under a bilingual banner reading: *Learn, Build, Belong.* None of it felt imported; it felt inevitable, like a memory the country had been waiting to recall.

By midsummer, the first Gateway City, still half cranes and scaffolds, already attracted tours. Journalists from Europe compared it to Scandinavian eco-districts; an American think-tank called it *"the world's first transparent economy in miniature."* Arjun preferred quieter language: "A place where the future can be fact-checked."

He knew skepticism would persist. It should. Trust untested is trust unproven. But each inspection, each audit, each click on the public dashboard was another thread in a stronger fabric.

At sunset one evening he stood with Evelyn on the ridge above the site. Below them, the new district glowed with temporary lights, a geometry of cranes and shadows. The wind carried the scent of wet earth and diesel.

"Do you think people will come?" she asked.

"They already have," he said. "Every worker, every family that moved here — they're the first citizens of belief."

The sun slipped below the tree line. In the distance, the rail line caught the last light like a drawn wire stretching east and west.

"This is how nations renew trust," he said quietly. "Not by slogans or speeches, but by building something that keeps its promises."

Evelyn watched the cranes swing slowly against the fading sky. "Then let's keep building."

When the wind shifted, it carried the faint sound of bells from the old downtown — church, city hall, fire station — each marking the hour in its own key. The new city below answered with its own lights, data pulses glimmering on screens. Old Canada and new Canada conversed across the valley, neither replacing the other, both necessary.

In that dialogue lay the definition of trust: continuity without complacency.

Trust is only as solid as the ground it stands on. The next test of the Gateway vision would be literal — how to translate faith into framework, belief into land. Canada's vastness was both promise and puzzle: whose soil, whose stewardship, whose share of tomorrow? To build cities of the future, they would have to start with the oldest question of all — ownership and belonging.

Every ideal must stand on ground.

7

INSIDE A GATEWAY CITY

The train curved north beneath a pale November sky, its windows streaked with the melt of early frost. Beyond them, the Sudbury basin opened wide — a landscape that had once burned under decades of smelter smoke now shimmered faintly with renewal. The horizon was a collage of memory and design: wind turbines where slag heaps had stood, solar towers rising from old quarries, and in the distance, the gleam of Ramsey Lake catching a low winter sun.

Arjun leaned forward, studying the city below. "It looks awake," he murmured.

Evelyn followed his gaze. "Or maybe it just remembered it was alive."

Five years earlier, this had been the first pilot site under the Canada Global Gateway Act — the law that turned intention into institution. It was not chosen by accident. Sudbury was once the economic heart of the nation — the city that mined the nickel which plated fighter jets, satellites, and pocket change. It had powered Canada's twentieth century, and then, as global demand shifted and automation arrived, it had fallen quiet. Half its young had left for the corridor between Toronto and Ottawa. Streets once full of miners' laughter now carried only the low hum of snowplows. If the new century was to rediscover courage, it had to begin where Canada's industrial heartbeat had slowed.

"Why Sudbury?" journalists had asked when the announcement came. The answer was pragmatic and poetic at once: because it had all the bones of a great city — and none of the vanity. Rail lines to two oceans. A skilled population. Space enough to build without erasing. And a culture forged by work — not entitlement. As one policy brief had put it, "Sudbury knows what it is to matter, and what it costs to stop."

When Arjun and Evelyn stepped off the train, the air smelled of pine and ozone. The old VIA Rail station had been repurposed into the Gateway Transit Hub, its copper façade etched with a motto in three languages — English, French, and Anishinaabemowin. Over the main doors was a short inscription: Land in stewardship, labour in dignity, prosperity in trust.

"Three promises," Evelyn said quietly. "If they keep even two, it'll change everything."

Outside, the city unfolded like a design. Downtown streets were narrower now, rebuilt for trams and bicycles. Roofs carried greenhouses; alleys hummed with heat exchangers drawing warmth from old mine shafts far below. What had once been called brownfield was now basestone — the foundation of a new energy grid.

Each district was a lesson put into practice. The Polytechnic Quarter rose where a refinery had once stood; its lecture halls shared walls with workshops and drone labs. The Cultural Corridor linked public art spaces to Indigenous cooperatives and a small amphitheatre overlooking the lake. Even the suburbs had changed form: clusters of mid-rise timber apartments were built around geothermal wells, connected by autonomous shuttle loops.

Arjun took all of it in, the quiet coordination between design and purpose. "It doesn't look futuristic," he said. "It looks finished."

Evelyn smiled. "Maybe that's the point. The future isn't a spectacle anymore. It's maintenance done beautifully."

They arrived at Tom Davies Square just as the Gateway Council convened its morning session. The building was glass and limestone, transparent by design: every meeting broadcast live, every vote timestamped and stored on the Gateway Public Ledger.

Inside, five members sat in a half-circle beneath a skylight rimmed with solar glass. At the centre was Naomi Michaud, an Anishinaabe economist who served as co-chair. To her left, a municipal planner from the City of Sudbury; to her right, a representative of the federal government, present in a strictly observer role. Two more seats belonged to industry and ethics representatives — one filled by a local clean-tech entrepreneur, the other by a public advocate elected online by residents.

"Five points of balance," Evelyn whispered. "No one gets to outvote the others."

The council agenda scrolled across a public screen: *Housing permits approved digitally; renewable-energy credit disbursement; quarterly mentorship ratios.* Each item carried a completion bar — green, amber, or red. The public could watch progress the way they watched weather.

Naomi opened the session with a phrase in Anishinaabemowin, translated in surtitles above her: *Good governance is a kind of civic ceremony: clear roles, clear rules, and a public that can see the promises being kept.*

she tapped her tablet, and the first bar shifted from amber to green.

"Decision logged," she said. "Twelve seconds."

Evelyn smiled. "That's faster than an Ottawa coffee line."

Later that day, they toured the old INCO lands, now the Renewal Basin. The iconic smokestack — once the tallest in the Western Hemisphere — was gone. Its metals had been melted to form the district's wind-tower frames, its site turned into a geothermal reservoir that warmed forty thousand homes. Around it, birch trees had reclaimed the soil.

A retired miner named Dario met them near the new energy control centre. His hands were thick, his voice soft. "We used to pull the wealth out of the ground," he said. "Now it grows on top of it."

Arjun asked how the transition felt. Dario shrugged. "At first, we didn't believe it. Thought it was another government slogan. But when the first geothermal cheques arrived, and my granddaughter got a scholarship at the Polytechnic — well, we stopped laughing."

The Sudbury Polytechnic loomed nearby, its façade of timber and glass gleaming against the sky. Inside, engineering students collaborated with trades apprentices on hydrogen-cell vehicles. A banner hung from the atrium: *Made in Sudbury — Meant for the World.*

Evelyn turned to Arjun. "This city isn't chasing relevance. It's practising it."

At the Polytechnic's training hub, they met Nina Roy, a twenty-two-year-old Canadian apprentice paired with an electrical engineer from India named Anoop Kumar. Together they were calibrating sensors for the city's micro-grid.

"Eighty-twenty," Anoop said with a grin. "She learns my tricks; I learn her slang."

The ratio — 80 percent foreign specialists, 20 percent Canadian residents — had been controversial at first. Yet the results spoke louder than opinion. Each specialist mentored one Canadian; renewal of their Gateway Employment Pass required verified mentorship hours and community engagement. Within ten years, the ratio was designed to invert — eighty percent domestic leadership drawn from those same apprentices.

Nina wiped grease from her hands. "My parents thought this program would replace us. Instead, it made me employable."

Evelyn nodded. "You're proving immigration isn't just a queue into Canada — it's a system for skills transfer, mobility, and contribution."

Behind them, a mural depicted a miner's lamp morphing into a wind turbine. Its caption read: *Work that teaches is work that lasts.*

In the afternoon, they were escorted to Gateway Fiscal Hall, a circular building overlooking the lake. Inside, a huge digital ring displayed live economic data — employment rates, emissions, energy output, tax receipts. The hall was open to the public, as required by law.

Luc Deschamps, the city's fiscal commissioner — a Métis economist known for his bluntness — welcomed them with a handshake.

"So, you want to know how we make generosity profitable," he said. "Simple: we don't give money away; we circulate it."

He pointed to the tax screen. Corporate income tax stood at 12 percent, but firms that reinvested locally — in housing, training, or R&D — could deduct up to half of their federal corporate income tax payable. Immigrant professionals received a three-year income-tax abatement if they mentored locals or launched start-ups within the zone. Every credit was time-bound and traceable through the Gateway Public Ledger.

Evelyn frowned slightly. "You're giving up revenue."

Luc smiled. "We're giving it forward. Every forgone dollar earns two back within seven years. We call it fiscal compounding."

Arjun studied the data: GDP up 11 percent, municipal debt flat, private investment tripled. Carbon credits from industrial retrofits funded free transit and a scholarship fund for Indigenous students.

"So it works," he said.

Luc shrugged. "When you treat trust as capital, it accrues interest."

Over dinner at a lakeside cafe, Evelyn flipped through her notebook. "So why here, really? Beyond the infrastructure?"

Luc leaned back. "Because Sudbury already knew what failure felt like. It didn't have to pretend humility. People here were tired of being studied. They wanted to build."

He listed the factors:

- **Geographic centrality**: Rail, road, and power grids already converged;
- **Social compact:** Strong unions, engaged Indigenous councils, cooperative governance;
- **Manageable scale:** Big enough to matter, small enough to learn from;
- **Cultural readiness:** Residents who understood that prosperity is borrowed — not guaranteed.

Evelyn jotted a note: *Transformation succeeds where ego sleeps.*

By dusk, the city's lights flickered across the water. Families strolled along the boardwalk; children skated on the first glaze of ice. The skyline glowed — modest, human, alive.

Arjun watched a tram glide past, its side panel displaying live metrics: *Zero-emission ride #82, Power source: geothermal 37 percent, solar 63 percent.*

"Imagine," he said, "a city honest enough to show its math."

Evelyn smiled. "Honesty might be the most Canadian innovation yet."

They stopped near a bronze plaque beside the lake. It bore the names of the city's first builders — miners, engineers, and students — beneath a simple line: *Renewal is a verb.*

Behind them, the wind carried faint music from an outdoor concert — a blend of fiddle and tabla, of old and new Canada finding a rhythm together.

Arjun turned to Evelyn. "Maybe this was never about proving we can build. It's about proving we can belong."

She looked out at the lights reflecting on the lake. "Belonging," she said, "and follow-through — the kind that turns welcome into a life."

Later that night, from the observation deck above Tom Davies Square, they watched the data halo — the heartbeat of a living experiment — rotate above the city.

Evelyn asked, "Do you think the rest of the country will believe it?"

Arjun thought for a moment. "They won't have to. Belief follows evidence. Once one city works, it stops being theory. It becomes precedent."

He looked down at the plaza where children were tracing patterns in the snow. "We built a city," he said softly, "but really, we built a mirror. It shows what Canada looks like when its values finally act like policies."

The wind lifted, carrying the low hum of turbines from the ridge. Evelyn closed her notebook.

"And what happens when the mirror spreads?"

Arjun smiled. "Then we stop calling them Gateways. We start calling them home."

Sudbury had been the first proof. It would not be the last. From coast to coast, applications for new Gateway charters began to flood Parliament's servers — not as petitions, but as blueprints. The frontier had found its new coordinates: fairness, purpose, and the quiet courage to build again.

8

THE ANATOMY OF A GATEWAY

By late June, Sudbury no longer looked like a mining town; it looked like a promise kept. The morning light pooled over Ramsey Lake, turning the water to silver glass. Wind turbines shimmered along the horizon, their blades cutting slow arcs through the bright air. The city that once carried the smell of metal and smoke now had the faint scent of spruce, coffee, and construction dust — the fragrance of work resuming with purpose.

It had been just over a year since the first Gateway broke ground, and the transformation was unmistakable. Where slag heaps once stood, gardens bloomed. The old rail yards thrummed again, this time with electric freight and commuter trams. Birch trees along the pedestrian boulevards flashed white in the sunlight.

Arjun Mehta stood on the terrace of the Gateway Civic Hall, a low-rise of timber and glass that overlooked the lake. He was dressed casually — open-collared shirt, sleeves rolled; his look when a plan had shifted from theory to life. Below him, the plaza hummed: students from Laurentian University in sun hats, Indigenous entrepreneurs from Manitoulin Island, recent arrivals from Lagos, Warsaw, and Manila, mingling in outdoor cafes and market stalls.

Evelyn approached carrying two iced coffees. "Do you realize," she said, shading her eyes with her hand, "that this is the first time in decades Sudbury's population has gone up?"

Arjun nodded. "Thirty-two thousand new residents since last spring. And it's not just an increase in numbers; there's a new mix of skills, cultures, and industries. It's like the whole world remembered where North Ontario is."

The Canadian Global Gateway Act, passed quietly the year before, had done what generations of policy papers couldn't: make prosperity visible. The Act authorized the creation of co-governed cities — shared ventures between municipalities, Indigenous councils, and the Frontier Trust. Each Gateway had to be financially self-sustaining and morally transparent, guided by the four coordinates Evelyn had etched years ago: Values, Discipline, Freedom, and Stewardship.

The funding structure itself was revolutionary. Every Gateway raised capital through Sustainability Bonds — green instruments backed not by taxes but by long-term land leases and productivity forecasts. Pension funds from Canada, Norway, and Singapore invested early. Sovereign wealth funds soon followed. It was the first infrastructure model in modern Canada that didn't drain the treasury. It replenished it.

Evelyn smiled, watching a group of children chase each other around the fountain below. "People still don't believe it worked without public money."

"It wasn't public money," Arjun replied. "It was public trust. The land stayed ours — the capital simply borrowed its potential."

Every lease in Sudbury carried two signatures: one from the Crown, another from its Indigenous partner. Ownership was collective; profit was shared. In a single design stroke, reconciliation became an economic structure.

Down by the lake, the Innovation Spine cut through the downtown — a sunlit corridor of labs, coworking lofts, cafes, and student housing. The old freight line had become a pedestrian greenway lined with smart benches, sensors, and solar trees that glowed softly at night.

Every building bore its own digital confession: small dashboard screens near the entrance displayed energy use, diversity ratios, and community contributions. Tourists stopped to read them the way they once read plaques on statues. Transparency wasn't paperwork anymore — it was part of the architecture.

Evelyn watched a tram glide past, its glass sides tinted blue like the sky. "They call it the world's first honest city," she said.

"It's really just the first city built on trust," Arjun replied.

And trust had delivered results. Unemployment had dropped from 8.3 percent to 3 percent. More than fifty new enterprises — from hydrogen storage start-ups to modular housing manufacturers — had set up within the first year. Wages rose. The city's small downtown cafes and hardware stores, long shuttered, were full again.

The 80:20 workforce rule, once a lightning rod of controversy, had proven itself beyond doubt. Eighty percent of initial technical roles were filled by foreign specialists who had obtained Gateway Talent Visas, designed for rapid entry and renewable every three years. Each visa holder was required to mentor a Canadian counterpart — knowledge transfer wasn't an option; it was a condition of employment.

Within months, apprenticeship programs tripled. By the end of Year One, over four thousand Canadians had upskilled, and seventy percent of foreign specialists had applied for permanent residency.

"It's not immigration," Evelyn said in a briefing once. "It's integration at design speed."

And it worked because it rewarded contribution — not just arrival. "He pointed to the tax screen. Corporate income tax stood at 12 percent, but firms that reinvested locally — in housing, training, or R&D — could reduce their effective tax by up to half. The reduction was governed by a simple reciprocity rule: for every dollar of tax relief claimed, three dollars had to be reinvested on the ground — payroll, apprenticeships, supplier development, community infrastructure. Immigrant professionals received a three-year income-tax abatement if they mentored locals or launched start-ups within the zone. Every credit was time-bound and traceable through the Gateway Ledger.

What looked like a loss to accountants turned into a gain for cities.

Toronto's real estate pressure finally eased. Housing prices plateaued as professionals began migrating north, drawn by Sudbury's new rhythm of work-life balance. Transit expansions, once stalled for years, now moved forward — and there were early talks to extend Highway 407 and 413 corridors northward, which would turn the Gateway into a two-hour commute from the GTA.

At sunset, Arjun would sometimes walk along the tramway to his home near the lake. That evening, the city glowed gold. Children played in the park. The hum of the electric buses mingled with street music. He could smell barbecue from an open-air restaurant — a smell Sudbury hadn't known in years.

At home, Anika set the table while Rhia spread out Arjun's papers. "So, this is what saved the North?" she teased, holding up a printed map of industrial plots.

Arjun laughed. "It wasn't saved. It's just started talking again."

Anika poured lemonade. "And the people who were here first?" she asked.

"They're leading it," he said. "Every Gateway lease begins with Indigenous signatures. Every school includes Indigenous curriculum. For the first time, reconciliation funds itself."

Tintin barked once, wagging his tail as if in approval. Rhia grinned. "Well, even he gets it."

They ate slowly as the sky turned amber outside the window. The city lights shimmered across the lake. Arjun looked at them — at his family, his city — and felt that peculiar satisfaction that comes when idealism finally finds engineering.

At the Civic Hall the next morning, Evelyn joined a delegation from the Frontier Trust. She wore a linen jacket instead of her winter coat, her sunglasses catching the glare off the polished steps. The delegates toured the digital dashboard room: a wall of living data streams showing energy flows, commute times, air quality, and employment ratios in real time.

Evelyn watched the figures, her reflection faint on the glass. "Maybe governance isn't slow," she said quietly. "Maybe it's just afraid of being seen."

Arjun turned. "Then it's time to show it how light feels."

Outside, the plaza shimmered. Banners for Frontier Week fluttered in the wind. A jazz trio played on the steps, and drones hovered discreetly above the construction sites along the southern ridge.

Sudbury had become more than a pilot — it was proof. A Canadian city reborn not through subsidy, but through self-belief turned into structure.

And in that sunlight, both of them knew — the next frontier wasn't just geographic anymore. It was moral.

The summer after the Sudbury Gateway opened, Canada looked north again.

News anchors who had once covered the region only during wildfires or strikes now led their broadcasts from its shining waterfront. Magazines called it "the city that reinvented Canadian capitalism." Economists called it "a case study in national self-correction." Evelyn called it something simpler: "proof that fairness and efficiency aren't opposites."

But behind the headlines lay the real story — one of structure, governance, and choice. Each Gateway City operated through a Tri-Council Charter. The three councils:

- Frontier Trust: a federal entity mandated by the Canadian Global Gateway Act;
- Municipal Authority: a body representing local citizens and businesses; and
- Indigenous Partnership Council: an organization ensuring land stewardship, cultural integration, and shared revenue.

The Tri-Council wasn't symbolic, it held binding powers. Decisions over land use, taxation, and environmental thresholds required a two-thirds cross-council majority. Each council could veto projects that violated sustainability or equity clauses.

It was governance as balance — not the old tug-of-war between bureaucracy and business, but a cooperative tension engineered to produce speed with conscience.

Evelyn often said the design borrowed its rhythm from nature itself. "Forests don't grow from one tree deciding everything," she told a crowd at the Civic Hall. "They grow because each part has its role — canopy, soil, root — and they share light."

That philosophy shaped every policy meeting. Ministers didn't sign off in Ottawa; they logged in. The Frontier Trust's Civic Interface Portal allowed public tracking of every project's life cycle — approvals, environmental reviews, construction milestones. Each step was timestamped, transparent, irreversible. The bureaucracy had been coded into software — transparent, time-bound, auditable — and suddenly delay was no longer defensible.

Of all the Gateway's mechanisms, none was debated more fiercely than the workforce ratio: 80 percent foreign specialists, 20 percent Canadian residents in the early phases. Critics called it demographic gambling. The press questioned whether it diluted identity. But Evelyn, armed with data, reframed it. "It's not an imbalance," she said on CBC's *Power & Politics*. "It's a starter culture — the way yogurt needs bacteria to ferment milk. Without external expertise, nothing transforms. But after fermentation, what remains is new and self-sustaining."

By Year Two, the results justified the metaphor.

Foreign engineers, designers, and data scientists who arrived via Gateway Talent Visas didn't replace local jobs — they multiplied them. For every foreign specialist hired, one Canadian apprentice was trained and one local contractor engaged. By the end of the second year:

- 4,000+ Canadians had completed technical apprenticeships;
- 70 percent of foreign specialists had applied for citizenship;
- 95 percent of start-ups incorporated within Canada;
- and 28 percent of new businesses were Indigenous-led.

The 80:20 formula had proven to be less a ratio than a relay, a structured passing of knowledge that turned migration into multiplication.

Rhia, now interning with the Gateway Planning Unit, called it "Canada's brain loop."

Skeptics had predicted massive deficits from Gateway tax incentives. But when the numbers arrived, they rewrote orthodoxy. For every dollar in tax reduction offered to corporations within the Gateway, the combined return to Canada's GDP was $4.12 — a ratio that startled even its architects.

How?

Because Gateway tax design rewarded reinvestment over extraction.

- Profits reinvested locally — in payroll, R&D, or equipment — were taxed at 12 percent.
- Profits exported abroad were taxed at 40 percent.
- Long-term leases (50–99 years) created continuous royalty streams split equally between federal, provincial, and Indigenous partners.

It was the first time Canada's fiscal architecture treated retention as a virtue. Arjun called it "a moral tax code" — one that aligned self-interest with stewardship.

By the second summer, Sudbury's local GDP had grown 24 percent year-over-year. Property values rose sustainably— not speculatively. The federal treasury collected $1.8 billion in new payroll and consumption taxes. And all of it — every project, every figure — was visible on the Public Performance Dashboard, accessible to any citizen with a phone.

For once, Canada's growth didn't need a press release; it had a live feed.

Every boom needs a reason to begin. For Sudbury, that reason arrived in the form of five anchor investments — each distinct, each catalytic, each a signal that the North was no longer a periphery but a platform.

NORTHERN ELECTRIC MOBILITY HUB (NEMH)

When the Canadian Global Gateway Act passed, global manufacturers were searching for secure, ethical supply chains for electric vehicles. Sudbury sat atop one of the largest nickel and cobalt deposits in North America — essential for battery production — but what convinced industry to move wasn't geology; it was governance. Under the Gateway's carbon-credit framework, any company manufacturing EV components within a certified clean radius (fifty kilometres powered by renewable grids) could offset 30 percent of its corporate tax against verified local employment. Within six months, a major automaker and EV supply-chain, LG Chem, and a consortium of Canadian cleantech firms established the Northern Electric Mobility Hub: a cluster of modular battery plants, recycling labs, and test tracks built on reclaimed mining land.

By the end of the second year:

- 7,200 new jobs were created;
- 80 percent of the workforce trained through Gateway apprenticeship programs;
- Emissions per manufactured unit were 64 percent lower than in comparable U.S. facilities.

Nickel that once left Canada as ore now left in high-value cells and systems. The North, long seen as extraction territory, had become fabrication territory.

GATEWAY ADVANCED MATERIALS CAMPUS (GAMC)

The second major anchor came from Siemens Canada and Hydro-Québec Technologies, who co-invested in the Gateway Advanced Materials Campus, a research and pilot-scale complex producing lightweight composites for aerospace and wind turbines.

The Campus operated as a public-private partnership between industry, Laurentian University, and the Frontier Trust. Students could earn micro-degrees while working alongside engineers in real-time production settings. GAMC alone added $1.4 billion to regional GDP and made Sudbury one of North America's leading suppliers of renewable infrastructure components.

NORTHERN CLOUD CORRIDOR

In a quiet valley east of town, what had once been an abandoned quarry was now the Northern Cloud Corridor — a cluster of hyperscale data centres powered entirely by hydro and wind energy.

The move began when Google Cloud Canada, Shopify, and NVIDIA AI sought a sovereign data environment compliant with both G7 and Indigenous data ethics. The Gateway's Data Reciprocity Clause, which required companies to share anonymized insights with public researchers, was the decisive factor.

Jobs followed knowledge: over 4,500 engineers, technicians, and cybersecurity analysts relocated to Sudbury. In cafes downtown, it wasn't unusual to hear Cree, Polish, Tamil, and JavaScript in the same conversation.

GREEN HYDROGEN BASIN

At the city's western edge, vast electrolysis fields shimmered under the sun, producing green hydrogen from Ontario's surplus hydroelectric grid. Funded through the Nordic Energy Partnership and co-owned by the Wabun Tribal Council, the Green Hydrogen Basin became Canada's first Indigenous-majority clean-energy export facility. Hydrogen was piped south through the upgraded 407 corridor, fuelling logistics fleets and freight convoys enroute to Toronto and beyond. By Year Three, the Basin alone was offsetting over two million tonnes of CO_2 annually, while returning steady dividends to both the local First Nations and the federal clean fund.

GATEWAY CIVIC SERVICES CLUSTER

Not all industries were industrial. Sudbury's fifth economic pillar was human: the Civic Services Cluster, which relocated thousands of federal and provincial digital–government jobs north. The Frontier Service Relocation Act, introduced quietly alongside the Canadian Global Gateway Act, incentivized Ottawa-based departments to move non-essential digital operations to new hubs. Sudbury became home to the National Clean Infrastructure Agency and the Centre for AI Ethics and Procurement Transparency. Each agency brought with it lawyers, coders, policy analysts, and administrators. Population diversity followed, as did cafes, daycare centres, and a surge in school enrolment.

Evelyn described it best during a press interview: "You don't need to invent new industries for a region — you just need to rehouse ambition where land and purpose meet."

By the second anniversary of the Gateway's opening, the job numbers told their own story:

- **Total employment growth**: +38,000
- **Median household income**: up 27 percent

- **City revenue increase**: +43 percent
- **Federal contribution**: net-positive $1.2B after incentive offsets

But perhaps the most profound result was psychological. For the first time in decades, young Canadians from Toronto, Windsor, and Vancouver didn't see moving north as exile — they saw it as opportunity.

Even Alberta took notice. In Calgary and Edmonton, mayors began lobbying the Frontier Trust to bring the model west. Alberta's energy base was ready; its industrial muscle eager for renewal. "If Sudbury can do it," said Calgary's mayor, "then so can the West. Let's build our own Gateway — but for carbon-neutral energy."

And so the map began to stretch again.

Infrastructure followed the momentum. Plans that had sat on shelves for decades were now revived — this time, financed privately through Frontier Infrastructure Bonds.

Highway 407's northern extension — once considered a fantasy — was now under construction, inching north toward the Sudbury Corridor. The province approved it after the *Gateway Logistics Report* showed it could carry both freight and green-transit lanes powered by hydrogen cells.

Further south, Highway 413's long-debated route was redesigned to link with the 407 extension — an unbroken arc connecting Toronto's industrial belt to Sudbury's innovation basin.

The Mississauga Line 10 Monorail, originally a municipal transit project, had found its second life as a Northern Connector — with feasibility studies exploring a future link to Sudbury via hybrid magnetic rail. For the first time, planners spoke seriously of a same-day commute between the GTA and northern Ontario.

At Toronto Pearson Airport, the Frontier Express Terminal — a dedicated customs and transit hub handling flights and cargo linked to the Gateway Cities — opened. Cargo once trucked overnight could now move by high-speed rail to Sudbury within five hours.

None of this cost the taxpayer a cent. The projects were funded through PPPs (Public Purpose Partnerships) — a modified version of public-private financing that tied investor returns to verified community outcomes — not speculative tolls. If a project didn't meet its employment or sustainability targets, bond yields dropped automatically. The incentives were moral, mechanical, and measurable.

When the first hydrogen-fueled freight convoy departed from Pearson toward Sudbury, journalists called it "Canada's green artery."

Evelyn, watching the live feed from her office, simply whispered, "At last."

By midsummer, Sudbury had stopped being an experiment. It had become a destination. Population surpassed 200,000 for the first time in its history. Cafes ran out of chairs. Schools reopened wings long shuttered. The Laurentian campus added programs in "Sustainable Systems Engineering" and "Ethical Urban Design." The most profound change, however, wasn't economic. It was cultural. Community fairs blended powwow dancers with jazz quartets. Filipino bakeries sold bannock beside croissants. Street names began to appear in both English and Anishinaabemowin.

One evening, Evelyn and Arjun stood at the newly opened Unity Square, where the flags of Canada, Ontario, and the local First Nations flew side by side. The plaza was filled with music and summer air.

"You know," Evelyn said, smiling, "when we started, people said this would split the country."

Arjun looked out across the crowd — laughing, trading, debating — and said, "They were half right. It split the past from the future."

The lights from the water danced on their faces. Above them, drones traced soft geometric patterns — part art installation, part data visualization of the city's energy flow.

From the speakers, a voice announced the next milestone: "Gateway West Initiative — Announcement Tomorrow, Calgary."

Evelyn turned to Arjun. "You're not slowing down, are you?"

"Canada's too big to stop at one success," he said. "The frontier moves west."

By late summer, the Gateway model had gone from pilot to phenomenon. Editorials called it "Canada's most successful experiment in intentional nation-building since the railway." Business schools built case studies. And in Edmonton, a single line from a televised panel sparked a movement.

Evelyn had been answering a question about scalability.

"Could this really work outside Ontario?" the host asked.

Evelyn paused, smiled faintly, and said, "The Gateway isn't a place. It's a principle. And principles travel faster than freight."

The next morning, Alberta called.

The premier's office in Edmonton had been watching closely. Alberta had weathered recessions, oil-price crashes, and a long identity struggle between energy past and energy future. Sudbury's rise — and its $4.12 return per tax dollar — was a wake-up call.

A week later, Arjun and Evelyn found themselves in a glass-walled meeting room overlooking the Bow River. The Calgary skyline gleamed against the Rockies, sharp and bright in the morning sun.

"We've got the pipelines, the talent, the capital," the premier said, leaning forward. "But the world doesn't believe Alberta can lead in clean growth. You proved Ontario could. I want the West to prove it better."

Arjun studied the map on the table — a stretch from Edmonton to Red Deer to Calgary, and further south to Lethbridge. Corridors of rail, power lines, and open land. He could see it instantly: a network of Gateways linked by energy, education, and enterprise.

"We don't replace your strengths," he said. "We repurpose them. What was once a pipeline can become a powerline."

Evelyn added quietly, "And what was once boom-and-bust can become build-and-balance."

Three months later, the Alberta Compact was signed — the second jurisdiction to join the Canada Global Gateway Network. Its foundation was a blend of Alberta's boldness and Ontario's structure: The Calgary Gateway Zone rose near the old freight yards of Alyth, designed for clean logistics, aviation biofuels, and AI-enabled manufacturing. The Edmonton Knowledge Commons turned former industrial space into a digital apprenticeship hub linking the Northern Alberta Institute of Technology, the University of Alberta, and Indigenous polytechnics. The Prairie Hydrogen Corridor connected Edmonton to Calgary with modular electrolyzer stations, using the same green-hydrogen technology first pioneered in Sudbury.

But Alberta wanted to do something more radical: combine energy independence with workforce renewal. The province negotiated an adapted 70:30 workforce model — still global in scope but tilted toward local trades and reskilling oilfield workers for renewable operations.

By Year One, fifteen thousand new jobs appeared in hydrogen production, precision agriculture, and construction.

The Canadian Global Gateway Act's fiscal model — taxing extraction at 40 percent and reinvestment at 12 percent — found a natural ally in Alberta's entrepreneurial culture. Corporations that had once hesitated to decarbonize now found they could profit from doing so.

The Alberta Clean Energy Federation, an industry coalition, reported record investment: $38 billion in the first eighteen months, 70 percent from private and foreign sources. None of it touched the federal balance sheet.

And yet, beneath the figures, something deeper was shifting: Alberta's sense of itself.

Evelyn had always said Alberta's greatest resource wasn't oil; it was confidence. In Edmonton, she stood before a crowd of former energy workers now enrolled in retraining programs. Behind her, a banner read, *New Energy for the Old Frontier.*

"Transition isn't about loss," she said. "It's about redefinition. The same hands that built the oil sands can build the turbines. The same engineers who designed refineries can design hydrogen hubs. Alberta doesn't need to change who it is — only what it powers."

The applause was long, not loud — the sound of pride rediscovering its footing.

At the Calgary site, Arjun walked through the hangar-sized fabrication halls of Gateway Aerospace Systems, a partnership between Bombardier, WestJet, and two Japanese investors. Rows of robotic arms assembled carbon-neutral aircraft fuselages. Hydrogen engines hummed softly on test rigs.

"You know," said the plant manager, "we thought you'd never convince Ottawa to support us."

Arjun smiled. "We didn't convince Ottawa. We convinced ourselves. Ottawa just followed the math."

The same day, another convoy left Sudbury carrying equipment for the new Prairie Hydrogen Corridor — proof that Canada's geography, once its obstacle, was becoming its engine.

Sudbury's success had started a chain reaction: Manitoba announced its Winnipeg Gateway for Agritech; Saskatchewan launched a Rare Earth Processing Zone near Prince Albert; British Columbia proposed a Pacific Data and Design Port near Prince Rupert.

For the first time in half a century, the national map felt balanced — not centralized. The federal report Gateway Impact Year 3 summarized it in simple figures:

- Five provinces engaged
- $186 billion private investment mobilized
- 2.3 million jobs (direct and indirect)
- Average GDP growth of 3.8 percent nationwide

But what mattered most was what it didn't measure — morale.

Small towns along Highway 11 that had been hollowed by migration were alive again. Universities saw their enrolment surge. Indigenous enterprises became some of the country's fastest-growing exporters.

When international observers from the OECD visited, they called it "a new model of federated prosperity."

Arjun called it something quieter: "Canada's next breath."

The third summer of the Gateway dawned over a Canada in motion.

On a humid July evening, Arjun, Evelyn, and a delegation of mayors gathered in Calgary's Gateway Plaza to mark the official launch of Gateway West. The air smelled of sage and grilled corn; a Métis fiddler played near the stage. A large screen behind them streamed live footage from Sudbury, where families were gathered at Ramsey Lake to watch the same broadcast.

Evelyn took the podium. "Three years ago, this idea began as a sketch — circles on a page. Now those circles are cities. And those cities are teaching us something that policy never could: purpose, once designed, becomes contagious."

Applause rose through the plaza.

Arjun joined her on stage. "Sudbury was the first. Alberta is the bridge. The next ones — out west, up north — will finish what our grandparents started when they tied this country together with rails and roads. This time, we're tying it together with reason."

He looked toward the horizon, where the sky flared orange over the Rockies.

"Frontier doesn't mean edge," he said softly. "It means beginning."

As the summer lights of Gateway West flickered across the prairie, the story shifted north again — to where land itself spoke before policy ever did. Because no Gateway, however advanced, could exist without an ancient foundation: the land, its keepers, and the covenant that made renewal possible.

9

LAND AND THE LEASE

The helicopter traced the curve of Hudson Bay, its shadow racing across ice flats that glimmered like broken glass. Below, a cluster of prefabricated cabins marked the edge of a survey grid — the first residential tract of a Gateway City that did not yet have a name. From this altitude, the cabins looked temporary, almost fragile, but to Arjun they were symbols of permanence. *People had come.*

When they landed, the air bit with salt and snow. Evelyn stepped out first, the wind tugging at her coat. "Imagine this in five years," she said. "Light rail, schools, a marina, homes built to last a century."

"Built to belong," Arjun replied. "That's the test."

They walked toward a row of markers where engineers were staking utilities. Each marker represented an idea older than the survey itself — ownership need not mean possession, and permanence need not mean purchase.

In the twentieth century, nations equated economic and social progress with the level of ownership of private property. Ownership was proof of freedom, and mortgages were citizenship made tangible. But the same system that stabilized old cities made new ones impossible. Speculation inflated prices; red tape froze supply. The result: abundance without access.

The Gateway framework turns that equation on its head. Land remains collectively owned — federal or Indigenous — while development operates through long leases. Enough time for families to build and businesses to plan; not long enough for speculation to calcify into monopoly. Each lease carries obligations as well as rights: maintenance, energy efficiency, community participation, and a modest renewal dividend that funds local education and healthcare.

For residents, a leasehold home costs roughly two-thirds the price of a freehold equivalent. For investors, the model offers certainty without surrender. For the nation, it ensures that land remains a public trust rather than a private inheritance.

Evelyn once described the lease model as "a handshake that outlives the hand." It allows continuity without feudalism — people build, improve, and bequeath, but the ground itself remains part of the common good.

At the planning office, a young analyst projected a 3D model onto the wall: terraced housing running down toward the bay, community greenhouses beside a geothermal plant, a circular market hall modelled after Inuit meeting spaces. "Every block renews its lease as a unit," she explained. "If you maintain the buildings together, the rate stays low. It rewards cooperation."

Arjun nodded. "Neighbourhood as fiduciary duty," he said. "That's new."

The economics were compelling. Traditional urban sprawl cost governments billions in redundant infrastructure; the lease system concentrated maintenance and made taxation predictable. Mortgage debt fell; savings rates rose. And because housing remained affordable, wage pressure eased without suppressing ambition. Employers could hire globally without importing inequality.

Foreign investors at first hesitated — ownership was their instinct — but soon discovered the advantage: a century of security with none of the political risk of permanent acquisition. Pension funds from Europe and Asia began to see leases not as limitation but as guarantee. The model spread like a quiet revolution — finance finally aligned with stewardship.

Yet the real innovation was cultural. The lease communities blurred the old boundary between immigrant and resident. Under the Employment Pass Program, up to 80 percent of the workforce in each Gateway City could be foreign specialists for the first twenty years, paired with a mandatory 20 percent Canadian complement. The ratio would gradually converge as skills transferred. Every worker, regardless of passport, paid full income tax from day one. Contribution replaced dependency as the measure of belonging.

To keep local hiring strong, the program linked employment passes to salary thresholds indexed to regional averages — an idea borrowed from Singapore's talent policy. High-skill jobs drew global experts; entry-level positions remained open to Canadians first. The balance ensured that opportunity lifted both groups simultaneously.

Those who stayed five years could apply for Gateway Residency, renewable and portable within the network of cities. Ten years of contribution earned an expedited path to citizenship. Integration was not charity; it was contract.

Arjun toured a construction site where crews were finishing a row of timber townhouses. The air smelled of resin and sawdust. A mason from Mumbai worked beside a carpenter from Moose Jaw, their conversation a mix of Hindi, English, and laughter. "Same tools," the mason said, holding up his trowel. "Different weather."

The supervisor handed Arjun a tablet displaying live statistics: local employment 22 percent; renewable-energy share 94 percent; safety incidents zero. "Everything's logged," he said. "Even the jokes get recorded somewhere."

Arjun smiled. "Good. Cities should remember how they were built."

Housing policy followed the same principle of fairness with flexibility. Residents could sub-lease units only through the civic exchange, preventing speculation and keeping prices tied to income growth. Each renewal cycle reviewed community metrics — education, energy use, public satisfaction — and adjusted lease fees accordingly. Good governance literally paid dividends.

To encourage permanence, the Community Pension Plan rewarded continuity. Workers who remained in a Gateway City for ten years accumulated bonus contributions; twenty years unlocked early-retirement options. The longer you stayed, the more your pension grew — and the greater the match from local revenues. It was loyalty translated into arithmetic.

Arjun explained it to a visiting journalist: "We're not trapping talent; we're anchoring it. People stay when staying makes sense."

In a town-hall meeting, a resident asked whether leasehold homes would feel second-class. Evelyn answered first. "You'll own every nail, every garden, every sunrise you see from the window. The difference is that the land you walk on belongs to everyone, including your grandchildren."

A pause followed, then applause. Ownership, it seemed, was expanding — not shrinking.

By fall, families had moved into the first completed block. Streets still smelled of new wood and paint. Children skated on the plaza's ice loop while drones traced delivery routes overhead. In the evenings, lights glowed through triple-glazed windows — warm squares against the Arctic blue. Each home bore a small plaque engraved with its lease term: *Commenced 2025 – Expires 2124 – Renewal Optional.*

Standing in the snow, Arjun imagined someone reading that plaque a century later. Would they see it as limitation or liberation? Perhaps both. The point was not to freeze history but to give it intervals — to force each generation to renegotiate responsibility.

The success of the housing model rippled outward. Universities proposed satellite campuses inside Gateway Cities, teaching renewable engineering and Arctic architecture. Global institutions saw opportunity: joint research centres, start-up incubators, innovation labs testing climate-resilient materials. Education became both anchor and export.

In one memorandum, a European rector wrote, "Canada has achieved what we tried to simulate — an economy where ethics and efficiency cohabit the same spreadsheet."

The same logic attracted technology firms seeking stability outside volatile markets. Data centres powered by hydro and wind offered secure connectivity; call-centre and analytics hubs found skilled bilingual labour; logistics companies used autonomous rail corridors to cut emissions. The zones diversified by design.

The leases also carried a quiet environmental clause: every square kilometre of developed land required an equal area designated for ecological restoration. The policy turned construction into conservation funding. "For every street we pave," Evelyn said, "we plant a forest." Satellite images began to show the pattern — green expanding with grey. Prosperity and preservation sharing the same footprint.

One visiting minister from Europe called it "the morality of symmetry." Arjun liked the phrase enough to write it in his notebook.

Still, skeptics remained. Some critics warned that leaseholds could deter long-term emotional investment; others feared administrative complexity. Arjun welcomed the debate. "Doubt," he told a conference in Vancouver, "is the down payment on innovation. Every reform pays it first."

He reminded the audience that the freehold model itself was an invention — useful for its time, inadequate for the next. In a century defined by climate change and migration, ownership had to evolve from absolute to adaptive. The Gateway leases were not anti-property; they were pro-posterity.

On a late-winter evening he met with a delegation of young engineers in a cafe overlooking the Ottawa River. One asked how the model would handle inheritance. Arjun drew a diagram on a napkin: concentric circles labelled *Family, Community, Nation.*

"The lease renews through contribution," he said. "If your children live here, work here, pay taxes here, they inherit automatically. If they leave, the home returns to the pool. Continuity tied to presence — not paperwork."

The engineer studied the sketch. "So, belonging is a verb."

"Exactly," Arjun said. "And verbs keep countries alive."

By spring, the government announced incentives for provinces to replicate the framework. Manitoba proposed a second site; Nova Scotia offered coastal land for an Atlantic Gateway. Private developers volunteered to adapt the model for affordable housing near existing cities. The lease had become a symbol — a quiet rebellion against speculation and stagnation alike.

Evelyn visited the original site before snowmelt. The sun hung low, washing the half-built skyline in gold. Workers waved from scaffolds. Children chased each other through drifts where streets would soon be paved. She thought of the plaque on every house: *Expires 2124 — Renewal Optional. Optional, but likely.* The country had rediscovered the habit of renewal.

In the end, the lease was never just a financial tool. It was philosophy rendered legal. It said that land is borrowed — not bought; that nations are partnerships between time and trust. It transformed ownership into stewardship, turning the oldest Canadian truth into the newest Canadian export.

As Arjun boarded the return flight, he looked down at the glinting roofs below. The first Gateway City was still young, its map barely inked, but already it told a story larger than economics. It proved that a people could share ground without losing footing; that freedom could wear the shape of fairness.

Above the clouds, the sun flooded the cabin with light. He opened his notebook and wrote a single line: *The frontier is not what we take — it's what we agree to keep together.*

Once the land had been spoken for, the harder challenge remained: deciding who would speak for it. Land could be mapped; authority could not. Arjun and Evelyn soon learned that speed without structure collapses, and structure without speed suffocates. The next frontier would not be physical — it would be procedural. Could Canada finally prove that democracy and decisiveness could coexist?

Land grants purpose; governance grants pace.

10

GOVERNANCE WITHOUT GRIDLOCK

The conference hall in Thunder Bay buzzed with a different kind of energy. Not the tension of politics or the haste of commerce, but the hum of coordination. Around a circular table sat an unlikely assembly: mayors, Indigenous leaders, federal administrators, entrepreneurs, and two dozen citizens selected by lottery. A screen on the wall displayed a live counter — *Permit Approvals Pending: 12 / Average Wait Time: 47 Days.* Beneath it scrolled a single motto: *Decisions are Public Goods.*

Evelyn leaned over to Arjun. "That counter — public shaming or transparency?"

He smiled. "Both. Accountability tends to multitask."

The meeting marked the first full sitting of the Gateway Council, the governing body of Canada's pilot economic zone. It was not a parliament, not a corporation, and not a municipal council in the traditional sense. It was a hybrid — the first institution in Canada designed to operate at the speed of private enterprise and the standard of public ethics.

Canada had long wrestled with bureaucracy's paradox: the more a system tried to be fair, the slower it became. Permits, consultations, audits — all noble safeguards — too often hardened into obstacles. The result was a kind of democratic exhaustion. People trusted institutions but dreaded interacting with them.

The Gateway model began by redefining bureaucracy itself. Instead of layers, it used loops — short feedback cycles powered by open data. Instead of gatekeepers, it used guardrails — rules that enforced standards without strangling initiative. And instead of departments, it organized around missions: housing, energy, mobility, education. Each mission had a cross-functional team that included at least one citizen member and one Indigenous representative, both with full voting rights.

Every policy draft moved through a digital workflow visible to the public. Anyone could trace its path from proposal to approval, timestamped and annotated. Silence longer than ninety days triggered auto-review; after 180 days, automatic escalation.

When skeptics complained that this sounded like technocratic utopia, Arjun countered with precedent. Estonia's e-governance reduced most permits to under a week. New Zealand published environmental approvals online before construction began. Even Dubai, for all its excess, mastered decision velocity. Canada could do the same — without losing its conscience.

He liked to say, "Efficiency isn't speed, it's respect for other people's time." A government that respected time was one that earned trust.

The Gateway Charter enshrined that respect in law. Section 6.4.3, known informally as the "Silent-Secretariat Clause," declared that the central secretariat no longer issued routine approvals. It only audited them. Routine tasks were delegated to automated workflows certified by human oversight. "If a decision requires only information — not judgment," Arjun told Parliament. "Let the machine decide — and let the human verify."

This shift startled traditional bureaucrats. Yet it freed them for what bureaucracy should have been all along: policy stewardship instead of paperwork custody.

Evelyn remembered the first time she saw the digital dashboard go live. A permit application pulsed green when complete, amber when delayed, red when flagged. Every citizen could see not only *what* was pending but *why*. The interface turned frustration into feedback. Complaints declined; collaboration increased.

"Transparency is cheaper than litigation," she noted in her planner. "And twice as fast."

Each Gateway Council meeting opened with a data review. Instead of speeches, charts. Instead of anecdotes, metrics. "Deliberation is still human," Arjun said, "but evidence sets the table."

To prevent capture by special interests, representation rotated. Citizen jurors served one-year terms, drawn by lot from the resident registry. Industry delegates rotated every three years. Indigenous councils appointed permanent envoys whose mandates outlasted electoral cycles, ensuring continuity without entrenchment. The effect was subtle but profound: no one owned the system long enough to bend it.

When disagreements arose, the council didn't adjourn; it voted in layers. Simple matters passed by majority; complex ones triggered a "cool-off loop" — seven days for public comment, then automatic re-vote. Deadlocks went to arbitration panels randomly selected from an independent roster of civic judges. Speed with second thoughts — a Canadian compromise made elegant.

Outside the council chamber, governance felt equally tangible. Digital kiosks dotted the city's public squares, allowing residents to check pending ordinances, comment on design drafts, or schedule community consultations. A young mother could renew her daycare license and vote on the new park layout between errands. Participation became an errand — not a crusade.

The backbone of this efficiency was the Open Ledger Network, a secure blockchain integrated with the national registry. Every land lease, utility bill, and procurement contract was recorded immutably, accessible to the Auditor General in real time. The old joke that government couldn't find its own files no longer applied; the files found themselves.

Arjun liked to explain the system with a metaphor: "Imagine a highway. Old bureaucracy sets up tollbooths; new bureaucracy paints lane markers." The goal wasn't to remove control but to make it continuous rather than episodic. Laws enforced themselves quietly in code, while humans reserved their energy for disputes that truly required judgment.

The model even redefined politics. Elected representatives within the Gateway Zones became stewards — not legislators. Their duty was to interpret community priorities within the charter's limits — not to invent new rules at whim. Campaigns were replaced by scorecards: performance metrics published at the end of each term. Popularity mattered less than reliability.

One commentator called it "post-partisan pragmatism." Another called it "bureaucracy with a heartbeat." Both were correct.

Critics warned that algorithmic governance risked coldness — in automating procedure, Canada might automate compassion out of public life. To guard against that, every automated decision came with a human-override clause. Any citizen could appeal to a live officer within seventy-two hours; if the officer reversed the algorithm, the system learned from the correction. Machine humility became policy.

Evelyn often said that compassion was simply "data with a pulse." The city's feedback loops tracked not only efficiency but empathy: response times to citizen inquiries, satisfaction scores, even linguistic inclusivity in public documents. Governance measured feeling as carefully as finance.

In practice, the results astonished skeptics. Business registrations processed in days — not months. Environmental assessments still rigorous but predictable. Infrastructure projects launched within a single fiscal year instead of spanning elections. The phrase "pending approval" began to disappear from Canadian vocabulary.

By the end of the first year, audits showed administrative costs 40 percent lower than comparable municipalities. Fraud detection improved; citizen satisfaction doubled. International delegations arrived to study the model. "You've made bureaucracy fashionable," joked a visitor from the OECD.

Arjun corrected him: "No, we made it functional."

Still, he insisted on humility. Systems age quickly. What begins efficient can ossify again if left unexamined. To prevent that, the Charter required a sunset review every ten years. Each rule expired unless explicitly renewed after public deliberation. Law regained mortality; relevance replaced permanence as the measure of legitimacy.

The first review loomed even before construction finished. Evelyn saw it as a reminder that progress was provisional by design. "Governance," she said, "should feel like gardening — prune what doesn't work, feed what does, and never let the system overgrow itself."

One evening, after a long council session, Arjun walked alone along the newly paved promenade. Streetlights dimmed automatically after he passed; wind turbines blinked red above the bay. He thought of the country he had returned to — a nation patient to a fault, allergic to haste — and smiled at the irony that its future might depend on acceleration.

He remembered Singapore's discipline, Finland's trust, and Canada's virtue. The Gateway model was their fusion: efficiency with ethics, rigor with reasonableness. If it succeeded, it would redefine how democracies worked in an impatient century.

He paused by a bench overlooking the frozen water. On a nearby wall a small plaque read*: Built by many, governed by all.*

He touched the cold metal and whispered, "That's it. That's the antidote to gridlock."

By spring, the council passed its first full budget entirely through the digital platform — three thousand citizens logged in live, watching the vote tally in real time. No closed doors, no last-minute amendments, no suspense beyond the democratic kind. It was messy, loud, and transparent. Exactly as it should be.

As the session closed, Evelyn addressed the assembly: "We've built the bones of a city that thinks for itself but listens to everyone. If we keep it honest, it might even teach the rest of the country to breathe again."

Applause rose, hesitant at first, then sustained. The data counter on the wall flicked to zero. *All permits processed.*

Outside, snow began to fall, each flake catching the plaza lights like static in the air — tiny, countless, orderly only in motion. The city was learning to move the same way.

Rules may keep order, but only inclusion keeps meaning. As councils formed and frameworks solidified, another voice grew louder — the demand to be seen. The Gateway blueprint could not simply manage participation; it had to embody it. The next chapter would test whether fairness could be engineered into foundation — not added in ceremony.

Systems serve no purpose without the people they include.

11

THE ARCHITECTURE OF INCLUSION

The meeting took place not in an office or hotel ballroom but in a longhouse made of cedar and glass, perched at the edge of a lake north of Sudbury. A thin mist rose off the water, blurring the line between reflection and sky. Inside, sunlight filtered through slats of wood, scattering across tables covered in handwoven cloth. Around them sat the people whose cooperation would decide whether Canada's boldest experiment would endure.

Evelyn laid out the blueprints: the transit line, the housing ring, the community square, the research centre. "Everything here," she said, "must be designed to include everyone who will live here — not as guests, not as tenants, but as partners."

An elder named Noah Whitecloud leaned forward. "Design is not enough," he said. "Inclusion is not about letting people in; it's about no longer imagining the place without them."

The Gateway Cities were never intended to be monocultures of efficiency. Their strength would come from coexistence — between the inherited and the invited, between the First Peoples and the latest arrivals. The architecture of inclusion began long before the first foundation was poured.

Every city charter contained what Arjun called the Fourfold Covenant: Respect for Rights, Recognition of Knowledge, Redistribution of Opportunity, and Reciprocity of Stewardship. Each word carried centuries of weight.

Respect meant Indigenous and local communities retained authority over land, language, and heritage. Recognition meant traditional ecological knowledge shaped environmental planning. Redistribution ensured that economic benefit flowed to those historically excluded from growth. And Reciprocity meant every partner — corporate, civic, or individual — had obligations as well as rights.

The process of translating these into detailed guidelines was not smooth. Negotiations stretched for months as legal teams argued over jurisdiction and revenue. Yet something rare emerged: agreement that inclusion must be a design principle — not a social program.

When the first framework was signed, it bore signatures written in Cree syllabics, English, and French. Noah Whitecloud stood beside Arjun and said quietly, "Now let's see if your buildings can speak all three languages too."

They could, and they did. Signs in the Gateway Cities appeared in multiple tongues. Public announcements alternated languages automatically. Even the city's AI assistants were trained on Indigenous phrasing patterns, ensuring that digital voices carried cultural cadence as well as syntax.

Evelyn loved that detail. "Our cities should sound like our country," she said.

Cultural integration went beyond symbols. The Indigenous Partnership Council held co-equal authority with the Municipal Council on all land-use decisions. Every lease renewal required a stewardship audit conducted jointly by Indigenous environmental officers and civic engineers. The audits didn't slow construction — they improved it. Problems that might have surfaced years later were caught at design stage.

An elder from Manitoba joked, "We used to get consulted after the damage. Now we get consulted before the design."

What began as reconciliation soon became collaboration, and finally, co-creation.

The city's physical layout embodied that idea. Instead of a single downtown core, planners built a constellation of Community Circles — mixed-use clusters of housing, schools, and small businesses surrounding shared cultural spaces. Each circle included an Elders' Pavilion, a Makers' Lab, and a Commons Garden irrigated by recycled greywater. The circles connected by tram and bike paths, forming a living mandala when seen from above.

"Cities usually grow like trees," Evelyn said, sketching the plan. "Ours will grow like coral — each part alive, each connected."

At night, the city lights formed patterns that mirrored the constellations above — a symbolic reminder that even the stars are plural.

The Employment Pass Program became another instrument of inclusion. Skilled immigrants from India, the Philippines, Nigeria, and Eastern Europe worked alongside Canadians from Alberta to Newfoundland. The workforce was multilingual, multi-faith, and remarkably cohesive. What bound them wasn't uniformity but purpose. They came not to extract but to build, and the city gave them ownership through responsibility.

The Gateway Fellowship Program paired every foreign specialist with a local apprentice, ensuring mentorship flowed both ways. Engineers from abroad learned winter logistics from locals; Canadians learned global trade from their peers. Knowledge moved faster than goods.

Arjun liked to say, "We don't import labour; we import leaders." It became a slogan, printed on banners at job fairs across Asia.

Inclusion also required equity in housing and access. Half of all residential units were designated "affordable by design" — construction materials, shared utilities, and energy systems made affordability inherent — not something achieved only through subsidy. Public transit was free for the first five years of operation. Digital connectivity was treated as a public right; every home had fibre-optic broadband and access to municipal cloud storage.

Schools followed bilingual curriculum, blending STEM (science, technology, engineering, and mathematics) with environmental science and Indigenous history. A single class might combine solar engineering, Cree geometry, and sustainable economics. "We're building a generation that understands stewardship as technology," Evelyn told a delegation of educators.

Still, inclusion demanded vigilance. When one private developer proposed a luxury enclave walled from the rest of the city, the council unanimously rejected it. "Walls," Noah Whitecloud said, "belong in stories — not cities." The decision set a precedent: exclusivity had no zoning category in the Gateway lexicon.

Arjun framed the rejection not as moral purity but as structural necessity. "Cities survive when their citizens share air," he said. "Segregation kills airflow, literal and civic."

To honour Indigenous stewardship, every Gateway City included a Sacred Trust Corridor — a band of preserved land running through the urban grid, managed by Indigenous rangers and open to all. The corridors protected migration routes, native flora, and ancestral sites. They also became the city's lungs, cleansing air and spirit alike. Tourists called them "urban sanctuaries." Locals called them "home."

The architecture itself reflected plural identity. Rooflines curved like waves or canoes; façades combined glass with cedar, steel with stone. Public art incorporated Métis beadwork patterns and modern LED installations. A plaza in the first Gateway City bore a sculpture of interlocking hands cast from copper, inscribed: *We built this together, and we stay together.*

No one could mistake these cities for foreign experiments. They looked — and felt — deeply Canadian.

Inclusion also shaped law. Legal reforms ensured that civic services adapted to cultural needs: multilingual contracts, gender-neutral documentation, and flexible faith accommodations. The judicial system included community mediation circles alongside formal courts. "Justice," Evelyn said during one session, "should sound like conversation before it sounds like verdict."

Childcare became part of this architecture of inclusion. Every primary school in a Gateway City was paired with an attached childcare centre, open from early morning until evening, designed to match the rhythms of working families. The service was universal and affordable, and for households where one or both parents worked full time — including single-parent families — the fees were refundable through the Gateway tax system. No parent was forced to choose between raising a child and pursuing opportunity. Inclusion meant designing cities that cared for the caregivers too.

Every new citizen signed the Gateway Covenant upon entry, a plain-language pledge affirming respect for Canada's Charter, Indigenous rights, and environmental stewardship. The Covenant didn't replace laws; it personalized them. People signed not just as residents but as custodians of a shared future.

When the first Festival of Light and Roots — a weeklong celebration blending Diwali, winter solstice, and Indigenous harvest traditions — opened, the city square overflowed with colour. Children danced around solar lanterns shaped like maple leaves; elders told origin stories beneath holographic constellations. A Filipino choir sang "O Canada" in four languages, the final verse in Ojibwe.

Arjun stood at the back of the crowd, humbled. "You can legislate policy," he said to Evelyn, "but you can't legislate belonging. That has to be earned."

She nodded. "And we're earning it one celebration at a time."

Over time, the cities developed their own accents — subtle blends of English vowels and Indigenous cadence, Arabic rhythm, and French melody. Food stalls offered bannock beside biryani, shawarma beside poutine. Children grew up tasting pluralism before learning the word for it.

Sociologists studying the Gateway experiment began to describe it as "applied multiculturalism." Not a mosaic, not a melting pot, but a living alloy — flexible, resilient, and luminous.

When Arjun spoke at the United Nations Forum on Urban Inclusion, he quoted Lee Kuan Yew: "A nation is great not by size alone. It is the will, the cohesion, the stamina, the discipline of its people." Then he added, "Canada has cohesion without conformity, discipline without dominance. Gateway Cities prove that fairness can scale."

The room stood in applause, not for rhetoric but for the proof behind it — a blueprint made visible in glass and timber, in streets named for poets and elders alike.

On the flight home, Arjun looked down over the faint lattice of lights stretching across northern Ontario. Each dot represented people who had chosen to build together — immigrants and locals, corporations and communities, First Peoples and newcomers. A living architecture, anchored in inclusion.

Evelyn, reading beside him, closed her notebook and smiled. "You realize," she said, "we're not just designing cities anymore. We're designing citizenship."

He turned toward the window, watching the aurora shimmer faintly across the horizon. "Then maybe," he said softly, "we've finally built something worthy of this sky."

Inclusion without livelihood is sentiment; inclusion with opportunity becomes citizenship. The Gateway model had to move from moral design to material dignity — jobs, wages, and wealth that stayed local. What began as dialogue about equity was now an equation of economics. Belonging, they would discover, has its own balance sheet.

Empathy acquires an engine.

12

THE ECONOMICS OF BELONGING

The evening sun spilled gold across the bay, turning cranes into silhouettes against a horizon of scaffolds and half-built roofs. From the balcony of the Gateway Fiscal Hall, Arjun looked down at a city under construction and thought: *This is what economics should look like when it belongs to people — not paperwork.*

Below, workers in high-visibility jackets laughed around food trucks. The rhythm of hammering and music mingled with the hum of machinery. The city was alive — not finished, but already functional. Prosperity had ceased to be theory; it had become sound.

The Gateway Economic Model was built on a single premise: inclusion, if designed properly, is not a cost but a catalyst. One of the clearest examples was childcare. By embedding early-learning and childcare centres into every primary school and reimbursing fees for full-time working parents — including single parents — Gateway Cities unlocked a portion of the labour force long sidelined by structural barriers. Economists called it the Participation Dividend: the measurable lift that occurred when new mothers and single caregivers re-entered the workforce months or years sooner than the national average. In Gateway Cities, childcare wasn't a social program; it was economic infrastructure. Traditional economics divided growth into winners and losers. Gateway economics merged them, converting social policy into market strength.

Every wage, every lease, every trade carried a feedback loop — measured, published, and reinvested. The objective wasn't redistribution through charity but through structure: the architecture of belonging.

Evelyn often said, "Inclusion isn't a subsidy. It's compound interest in human form."

The financial core of each Gateway City operated on four interconnected engines: revenue stability, workforce participation, investment incentive, and consumption growth.

Revenue stability came from lease fees and predictable taxation rather than speculative property cycles. The lease model turned what was once volatile land revenue into long-term annuity streams. Municipal budgets finally breathed in decades — not quarters.

Workforce participation was maintained through the 80/20 employment ratio — 80 percent skilled foreign specialists and 20 percent Canadian residents in the early decades — ensuring both expertise import and local uplift. The system produced what economists called "circular capacity," where skill transfer continuously replaced dependency.

Investment incentive flowed through the Gateway Inclusive Incentive Initiative (GIII) — a dynamic tax framework rewarding reinvestment and longevity. New immigrants and investors received temporary rebates: 30 percent for the first two years, 25 percent for years three and four, and none thereafter. The incentive wasn't a loophole; it was a runway.

Consumption growth came naturally. As residents earned, built, and settled, they consumed locally — housing materials, education, healthcare, leisure — all inside the lease ecosystem. The multiplier effect doubled the velocity of money while halving leakage.

When questioned in Parliament, Arjun summarized the model simply: "We don't chase capital. We cultivate confidence. And confidence is the world's rarest currency."

Confidence required proof. Within a year, Gateway Cities published transparent fiscal dashboards: tax inflows, payroll data, energy costs, export volumes. Every citizen could see the city's balance sheet live. Instead of mystery, there was math. Instead of rumour, results.

The GIII became the city's most talked-about innovation. It applied both to individuals and corporations, scaling benefits with contribution. For individuals, the Gateway Income Tax Rebate smoothed financial adjustment during their first years in Canada. Skilled migrants could save more initially, allowing them to settle without debt. By Year Five, their rebate expired — but by then, most had invested in property leases, education, or local businesses.

For companies, the incentive rewarded reinvestment: profits reinvested locally received tax credits; profits expatriated did not. The policy flipped the psychology of foreign direct investment. Foreign firms came not for extraction but for establishment.

A senior economist from the OECD wrote in a review, "Canada's Gateway model treats taxation not as punishment but as partnership."

Modelling by the Department of Finance projected short-term revenue deferrals of 10–12 percent — well within sustainable thresholds. Yet the same models forecast 200 to 300 percent growth in consumption, lease income, and trade duties over five years. The Gateway Network was designed like a flywheel: slower to start, unstoppable once spinning.

The data proved it. Retail activity in the first pilot zone exceeded projections by 40 percent within eighteen months. Average lease renewals hit 92 percent. New business registration time dropped to four days. Investors weren't fleeing Canada — they were forming queues.

For workers, the economy offered something they hadn't seen in years: security without stagnation. The Community Pension Plan (CPP+), integrated into every lease-based employer agreement, rewarded continuity. Workers who stayed in a Gateway City for ten years earned a 10 percent pension bonus; twenty years, 20 percent; thirty, early retirement. The plan was jointly funded by payroll levies and municipal revenues.

Arjun explained the logic during a televised interview: "People move where they're needed, but they stay where they're valued. If you want to build cities that last, give permanence a paycheque."

The Gateway model also aligned with national fiscal prudence. Because foreign specialists paid full income tax from day one, and because all earnings flowed through domestic banks, the federal government gained reliable inflows from day one. These revenues, combined with rising consumption and reduced unemployment insurance costs, more than offset initial incentives.

Evelyn joked, "It's the first immigration policy that pays for itself faster than it prints forms."

Behind the humour was truth: the model turned newcomers into net contributors immediately.

Financial inclusion extended to credit access. Gateway banks operated under a micro-macro hybrid system: residents with short credit histories could leverage community lease equity as collateral. Every year of residency increased a "trust score" that replaced traditional credit ratings. Default rates dropped below national averages. Immigrants who once spent years proving solvency now entered mainstream finance within months. One local banker described it succinctly: "We replaced credit history with civic history."

At city scale, trust became tangible in fiscal metrics. The Gateway Treasury Authority — a lean, algorithmically assisted agency — published real-time dashboards of tax collection and expenditure. Citizens voted annually on a small discretionary fund, allocating up to 5 percent of the surplus to community projects. One year, they chose a new ice rink; the next, a research grant for battery recycling. Taxes stopped being invisible extractions; they became visible investments.

Every financial report carried a note at the bottom: "Transparency is the dividend of democracy."

Still, the true genius of the Gateway economy was its resilience. By leasing land instead of selling it, cities avoided speculative bubbles. By linking incentives to reinvestment, they created recurring capital loops. By tying pensions and credit to residency, they built loyalty that could not be legislated. A lease is not a loophole around ownership; it is a covenant of stewardship — a structure that keeps land productive without letting speculation fragment its purpose.

Economists called it "Circular Capitalism." Arjun preferred a simpler phrase: an economy that remembers who built it.

In a meeting with federal ministers, one skeptic asked if the model could scale beyond experimental cities. Arjun replied, "Of course. Canada already does long-term leases in every national park and federal port. We're just extending that logic from conservation to civilization."

That line made the evening news. Headlines the next day read: "From Parklands to Promises: Canada Reinvents Ownership."

Foreign analysts took notice. Singapore's sovereign funds studied the model for replication; India expressed interest in partnership; several Middle Eastern investors proposed joint-venture logistics corridors connecting Gateway ports to global markets. The U.S., still tightening its H-1B visa programs, began quietly exploring Canadian alternatives.

Arjun knew timing was everything. "The world is full of talent with nowhere to go," he said. "Canada has space, safety, and sincerity. We just have to open the door wide enough."

And the world began to knock.

To protect integrity as investment flooded in, the Gateway Financial Code imposed strict transparency: no anonymous holdings, mandatory ESG (environmental, social, governance) audits, and profit-sharing with civic funds. The effect was immediate — ethical capital found a home; speculative money looked elsewhere.

The code wasn't anti-business; it was pro-future. "We don't need every investor," Evelyn said. "We need the right ones."

By Year Three, the economic landscape around the pilot Gateway had transformed. Local unemployment fell to record lows. Indigenous enterprises reported revenue growth of 120 percent. Women-led start-ups tripled. Secondary industries — education, healthcare, logistics, culture — flourished. GDP per capita in the region outpaced the national average by 40 percent.

Analysts coined a new term: "The Belonging Premium" — the measurable economic uplift created when citizens feel ownership of outcomes. Happiness surveys and spending patterns converged. Trust had become a leading indicator.

At a global economic forum in Geneva, Arjun summarized the transformation: "We used to think belonging was sentimental. Now we can calculate it. Every act of inclusion compounds; every structure of fairness attracts capital faster than any tax cut. The most stable societies are not the richest; they're the ones that share their future most convincingly."

In the first Gateway's civic square, a bronze plaque was unveiled that read: *Prosperity belongs to those who build it together.*

The inscription faced the water, reflecting sunlight across the plaza. Children played nearby; cafes buzzed with conversation in five languages. The air carried the smell of coffee, timber, and fresh concrete — the scent of an economy reborn not by chance, but by choice.

Evelyn watched the scene and turned to Arjun. "Do you ever think this could have failed?"

"Every day," he said. "That's what keeps it honest."

By nightfall, the lights of the new city shimmered on the bay, mirrored in the calm water. Each reflection doubled the sense of promise. To anyone looking from above, it was just illumination. But to those who lived here, it was proof — inclusion could pay dividends, belonging could be budgeted, and fairness could, finally, fund itself.

Prosperity that ignores the planet is poverty postponed. As investment poured in and the first districts rose, the conversation turned skyward — to air, water, and endurance. The measure of success would no longer be output alone but the footprint left behind. The Gateway experiment now had to breathe clean.

Belonging shapes a society; stewardship sustains a civilization.

13

SUSTAINABILITY AS STRATEGY

The wind off Lake Superior carried a low hum through the turbines on the ridge. Each blade cut the air with patient rhythm, turning light into power, motion into meaning. From the observation deck, Arjun watched the city below: streets bright with electric buses, rooftops glinting with solar glass, vapour rising from geothermal vents like steam from a living organism. The Gateway experiment had matured into something larger than economics. It had become proof that climate stewardship and competitiveness could share the same sky.

Evelyn joined him, gloves tucked under one arm. "You realize," she said, "we've built an economy that breathes."

He nodded. "And it exhales profit without pollution."

Sustainability had been woven into the Gateway DNA from its first sketch. Every metric — taxation, employment, housing — carried a carbon variable. Success wasn't measured only in GDP or jobs but also in carbon intensity per capita and energy return per unit of emission.

Each city was energy-positive by charter. Rooftop solar, on-site wind, hydro micro-grids, and waste-heat capture combined to generate 120 percent of local demand. Excess fed the national grid, turning new cities into power exporters. Factories paid differential tariffs tied to emissions: the cleaner the process, the lower the bill. Green arithmetic replaced greenwashing.

Evelyn's engineers called it the invisible economy of air. Every ton of carbon saved appeared on the public dashboard beside tax revenue, reminding residents that sustainability was not charity — it was currency.

The principle, often voiced by modern economists and environmental financiers, is that true prosperity aligns economic value with human values. The Gateway Cities made that philosophy tangible. Each investment carried a dual mandate — financial return and social responsibility — audited quarterly. ESG reporting wasn't optional; it was embedded in code.

The Gateway Green Bond Facility issued instruments benchmarked not by interest but by impact. Bonds earned premium rates when environmental targets were exceeded. Pension funds, insurers, and sovereign investors joined eagerly; ethics, finally, had yield.

At an investor summit in Montreal, Arjun summarized the shift: "We've replaced quarterly anxiety with generational arithmetic. Capital is patient when conscience is profitable."

The audience rose in applause. Carney, watching from the front row, smiled slightly with the rare satisfaction of seeing theory find steel and soil.

The industrial park south of the bay looked ordinary until you followed the trucks. Nothing left empty. Waste from one process became feedstock for another — aluminum scraps to additive-manufacturing plants, organic residues to biogas digesters, glass shards to composite facades. The system looped like a living circuit.

"Nothing unused, nothing unaccounted for," the operations manager said. Even the city's sewage was processed into fertilizer pellets branded *Gateway Green*. Circularity had gone mainstream.

By 2035, projections showed Gateway Cities reducing national carbon intensity by 35 percent — a figure that turned heads in global climate negotiations. Canada, once seen as a reluctant environmental player, began exporting clean-governance models instead of crude oil.

Public transport followed the same ethos. The SkyLoop, an elevated electric-bus network, glided silently above main roads. Beneath it, autonomous shuttles served neighbourhoods; cyclists used heated lanes that melted ice through geothermal coils. Freight moved at night on hydrogen-powered rail to keep days quiet for residents. Mobility became choreography — not congestion.

Every vehicle shared data with the city's carbon ledger. Commuters could track the emissions they *didn't* produce, displayed on monthly statements beside tax credits. Sustainability became visible, gamified, proud.

Architecture turned environmental constraint into creative brief. Buildings oriented themselves by sunlight and wind; façades breathed through micro-vent panels; timber replaced concrete wherever feasible. Construction waste dropped by 80 percent. Rainwater harvesting lined every roof. The skyline shimmered less from glass than from intelligence.

A visiting delegation from Japan called the aesthetic "northern modernism with conscience." Evelyn preferred a simpler phrase: "Form follows future," she said. "Design for the Canada we're becoming — not the Canada we used to be."

Each new district included carbon gardens — reforestation plots integrated into the urban fabric. Children planted trees on their birthdays; companies sponsored restoration instead of billboards. The more the city grew, the greener it became.

Power generation in the Gateways was decentralized. Instead of one utility monopoly, micro-grids allowed residents to trade energy credits peer-to-peer. A family with surplus solar sold directly to a neighbour's heat pump. Blockchain authenticated every transaction. It was capitalism at the speed of sunlight.

The result was resilience. During a winter storm that blacked out parts of Ontario, the Gateway grid rerouted seamlessly, keeping hospitals and homes powered. Headlines read: "When the lights went out, the future stayed on."

Arjun later told Parliament, "We've proved that green systems aren't fragile — they're flexible."

Net-zero wasn't just an environmental target; it was a market framework. The Carbon Dividend System priced emissions at source and recycled revenue directly to citizens through energy rebates. Polluters paid; participants profited.

Companies exceeding efficiency benchmarks received tradable Green Performance Credits (GPCs), redeemable for tax offsets or infrastructure bonds. By Year Five, GPC trading rivalled traditional commodity markets in volume.

Critics feared complexity. Arjun responded, "Complexity is confusion without transparency. Ours is transparent." The online dashboard showed every credit created, traded, or retired. The planet finally had a paper trail.

Evelyn argued that sustainability wasn't just technical — it was emotional. "You can't protect what you don't love," she told a conference of urban designers. To nurture that affection, every city wove art and ecology together: sculpture gardens powered by kinetic wind, amphitheaters doubling as flood basins, parks named after rivers rather than donors.

Even public festivals adopted circular practices. The Festival of Light and Roots ran on reclaimed biofuel; waste was composted within forty-eight hours. Children designed murals from recycled metals.

"We're raising a generation," Evelyn said, "that will treat climate neutrality as common sense."

The Gateway framework attracted unexpected allies. First Nations energy cooperatives managed wind farms under shared-ownership models. European climate funds financed district heating in exchange for carbon credits. Asian technology firms provided battery innovations in return for residency permits. Global cooperation replaced global competition.

At the COP 31 Summit, Canada unveiled the Gateway Protocol — a set of guidelines for ethical industrial zones worldwide. Delegates from forty countries signed on. For the first time, a Canadian policy document received standing ovation on an international stage.

Inside the Resource Recovery Complex — a cathedral of recycling on the city's western edge — robots sorted plastics by polymer, shredders hummed like choirs, and conveyor belts moved with clockwork grace. Above the noise hung a banner: *Nothing Lost, Everything Learned.*

Here, innovation met humility. The city's own waste funded start-ups experimenting with bio-resins and carbon-capture cement. The garbage truck became a research vehicle. The landfill era quietly ended.

Evelyn liked to remind visitors, "Every bin is a lab if you design it right."

For residents, sustainability translated into savings. Energy bills were 40 percent lower than national averages. Public transit was free. Health indicators — respiratory illness, heat stress — fell dramatically. Property values rose — not from speculation but from stability.

Arjun called it *the human dividend* — proof that prosperity measured in well-being is still prosperity.

At an evening forum, a student asked Arjun, "Do you really think capitalism can be moral?"

He paused before answering. "Capitalism isn't moral or immoral — it's a tool. What matters is who holds the handle. We built a system where conscience and competition finally pull in the same direction."

He gestured toward the skyline — wind towers blinking in synchrony, solar façades glowing amber. "That's what Mark Carney meant when he wrote that prosperity must rest on moral purpose. We just added a power grid to it."

The ripple spread far beyond the pilot zones. Provinces began retrofitting existing towns with Gateway energy systems. Mining companies adopted green-bond financing to maintain access to export markets. Universities overhauled curricula to include climate accounting and sustainable engineering. Canada's carbon footprint fell even as its GDP rose.

Economists coined a new phrase: "The Canadian Decoupling." Growth without guilt. Profit without penalty.

Foreign students began citing the Gateway experiment as a case study in moral modernization — a nation rediscovering ambition through restraint.

Late one night, Evelyn walked alone through the city's Eco-District. Snow crunched underfoot; wind turbines turned slowly above. She passed a row of streetlights whose glow shifted warmer as she approached, saving energy through proximity sensors. At the corner, a digital sign displayed the city's live carbon balance: –2,478 tons CO_2e this month.

She stopped, smiling. Negative emissions — literal progress. The sign blinked a line of text across the bottom: "Thank you for breathing with us."

She thought of all the countries she'd studied, all the plans she'd drawn, and felt something deeper than pride. It was gratitude — to be alive in a place that proved sustainability wasn't sacrifice but synthesis.

The next morning, the federal cabinet approved the expansion of the Gateway Network nationwide. The prime minister addressed the nation from the House of Commons: "We have learned that leadership in the twenty-first century is not about choosing between the planet and prosperity. It is about proving they are the same pursuit."

Arjun watched the broadcast from the construction site, hard hat under his arm. Around him, cranes moved like slow-motion punctuation marks against a sentence the country had just finished writing.

He turned to Evelyn. "Do you think we've finally aligned value with values?"

She smiled. "Maybe. But remember — alignment needs maintenance."

They laughed, and the wind carried their voices over the rooftops, blending with the steady hum of turbines.

The Gateway Cities stood now as living testaments to an idea once thought impossible: a nation could open its frontiers to the world, invite industry without injury, and make sustainability its most profitable export.

In the glow of evening, the skyline seemed almost weightless, as if the Earth itself were exhaling relief. Canada had found its rhythm again — patient, purposeful, and finally in tune with its own conscience.

Out of conservation came creativity. Efficiency bred invention. With energy grids stabilized and waste streams closed, a new hunger appeared — the drive to build smarter, faster, lighter. Sustainability was no longer restraint; it had become springboard. The next movement would explore innovation not as novelty, but as continuity.

To sustain is to keep creating.

14

THE INNOVATION CONTINUUM

Morning light flooded the Innovation District — a grid of glass-and-timber buildings arranged around a square where students, researchers, and entrepreneurs mingled over coffee and code. The smell of roasted beans drifted from a cafe run by former engineers from Mumbai; across the plaza, a 3D-printing lab buzzed as robotic arms sculpted prototypes from biodegradable polymers. Arjun watched the scene from a balcony above and smiled. "This," he said to Evelyn, "is what optimism sounds like."

The Gateway Innovation Continuum wasn't a program, it was an ecosystem — designed to blur the boundaries between academia, enterprise, and everyday life. It connected the research lab to the factory floor, the classroom to the boardroom, the immigrant's visa to the investor's vision. It was Canada's declaration that invention would no longer be an afterthought, but the operating system of growth. The principle was simple: build environments where the cost of experimentation was lower than the cost of hesitation.

Each Gateway City housed a Triad of Creation: a university satellite campus, a government-funded innovation lab, and a private accelerator.

Together, they formed the Innovation Continuum Cluster (ICC) — a 24/7 engine of ideas.

Students could develop prototypes with industrial mentors; corporations could test sustainable processes in live factories; start-ups could access data sandboxes without months of red tape. Intellectual property generated inside the cluster belonged jointly to creators and the community. The rule was explicit: *invention profits everyone or no one.*

Arjun called it "the most Canadian form of capitalism — collaborative."

At the northern edge of the city stood Gateway University, its motto carved above the entrance: *Learn. Build. Belong.*

The university didn't resemble a traditional one. Lecture halls doubled as maker spaces; professors worked alongside entrepreneurs; students received academic credit for launching start-ups or solving municipal challenges. Degree programs blended disciplines — engineering with ethics, economics with ecology, data science with diplomacy.

A visiting scholar from MIT remarked, "You've turned education into public infrastructure."

Evelyn responded, "Exactly. Knowledge should have footpaths — not fences."

The start-up ecosystem thrived on inclusivity. The Gateway Seed Fund, capitalized by both public and private investors, offered equity-free grants for early-stage ventures tackling challenges in clean energy, food security, fintech, and social innovation. Applications were processed through a live digital platform, with transparent scoring and public feedback. The only competition was quality.

Every funded start-up received access to co-working labs, legal templates, cloud infrastructure, and mentorship from the Global Enterprise Network (GEN) — a volunteer consortium of Canadian expats from Silicon Valley, Singapore, and London. For the first time, the global brain drain began to reverse direction.

One of the Continuum's most powerful tools was the Innovation Employment Pass — a streamlined visa for entrepreneurs and researchers who brought intellectual property rather than just capital. Applicants received immediate residency in a Gateway City, workspace in an ICC cluster, and access to seed capital if their projects aligned with the city's sustainable goals.

Unlike traditional immigration systems built on quotas, the Gateway model operated on merit and mission. A software engineer from Lagos, a biomedical researcher from Seoul, a robotics student from Calgary — all could join the same ecosystem within weeks.

By Year Three, the Gateway Cities hosted more than forty thousand innovators representing 120 nationalities. Canada's diversity, long celebrated, had become its superpower.

Inside the Advanced Manufacturing Campus, industrial robots worked beside apprentices. Each production line had a research terminal connected directly to the nearby university. Students could tweak algorithms and watch machines adjust in real time.

The result: a perpetual feedback loop between research and production. When a start-up designed a new sensor, the factory printed and tested it the same day. When a student developed an AI model to optimize power usage, it deployed within hours. Innovation moved at the speed of iteration.

Evelyn often joked, "We turned the city into a science fair with payroll."

The Continuum's most radical policy was its treatment of data. In most nations, data belonged either to corporations or governments. In Gateway Cities, it belonged to the Civic Data Trust — a publicly governed repository where anonymized information from transport, energy, and commerce was shared for research and entrepreneurship.

Start-ups could access datasets through open APIs, provided they adhered to strict privacy and reciprocity rules. In return, they contributed insights back to the Trust. The loop made data not a commodity but a commons.

Arjun described it as "the world's first ethical data economy." Investors called it "predictable innovation." Citizens simply called it "fair."

Innovation needs freedom, but freedom needs guardrails. The Continuum introduced the Ethical Innovation Code, developed jointly by lawyers, ethicists, and technologists. Every new product or process underwent a quick, transparent ethics review assessing safety, fairness, and environmental impact. Approval took days, not months — but the oversight was real.

Failures were public — not punished. Start-ups that stumbled shared lessons openly, creating what locals called the "failure dividend." Mistakes became mentorship.

"Only a confident society can afford to learn in public," Evelyn said at a press briefing. "And we're finally that confident."

The 50–99-year land lease model extended to industrial space. Companies leased labs — not land. In return for stability, they contributed 1 percent of revenue to the city's Innovation Reinvestment Fund, financing education and start-ups. The effect was elegant: each success literally paid forward the next generation of innovation.

One economist wrote, "The Gateway system turns capitalism into a relay race — every sprinter passes the baton."

Partnerships multiplied. A German automaker launched a battery lab beside a Canadian mining firm. A Singaporean university opened a joint AI centre. Indian pharmaceutical companies partnered with local biotech labs to test sustainable production. Gateway's time zone overlap — between Europe, Asia, and the Americas — made it a natural bridge for global collaboration.

Even Silicon Valley took notice. A major U.S. tech firm announced it would relocate its cloud research team to a Gateway City, citing "talent diversity, energy costs, and quality of life." The *Wall Street Journal* headline read: "The World's Next Tech Capital May Be North."

By Year Five, measurable outcomes exceeded projections. Start-ups per capita tripled national averages. Patent filings grew 400 percent. Export revenue from high-tech manufacturing surpassed natural resources for the first time in Canadian history.

But the real victory was cultural. Failure lost its stigma; invention regained its dignity. Immigrants became employers; apprentices became inventors. The economy no longer depended on luck or location — it depended on curiosity.

At the Gateway Innovation Awards, Arjun stood before an audience of scientists, founders, and community leaders. "Innovation," he said, "isn't about chasing the new — it's about keeping promises to the future."

The crowd stood in silence, then broke out in applause.

Evelyn's team built the Living Lab District — a neighbourhood where every building, vehicle, and appliance doubled as a sensor. Energy flows, traffic density, waste cycles, even water quality, all visible on a single dashboard. Residents voted on which experiments to approve: self-heating sidewalks, algae-based air filters, vertical farming towers.

It wasn't a test site; it was a community with innovation built on consent. The line between citizen and scientist vanished.

When a prototype solar pavement project succeeded through a local start-up, it was replicated across Europe within two years. A grandmother from Sudbury wrote in a letter to the editor of a local newspaper, "We used to export lumber. Now we export sunlight."

For Arjun, the Continuum's most profound achievement was not technological but psychological. It restored Canada's confidence. A nation once known for caution had learned to take creative risks without losing kindness.

He recalled reading: "Markets must be grounded in humanity." In Gateway Cities, markets were powered by it.

At a cafe overlooking the plaza, Evelyn asked, "Do you think we'll ever run out of ideas?"

Arjun looked around — the drones overhead, the laughter below, the murals glowing with LED art. "Ideas? Never," he said. "Only excuses."

The federal government soon announced the National Innovation Corridor, linking Gateway Cities by high-speed rail and data fibre, allowing clusters to share research in real time. The network extended from Halifax to Vancouver, passing through the heart of the country. For the first time, innovation moved faster than politics.

Canada had found its next identity: pioneer. The quiet country had learned to speak in patents and prototypes.

As night settled, the Innovation District glowed softly — the light of screens, labs, and late ideas. From her office, Evelyn watched students leaving the labs, their laughter echoing across the square. She whispered to herself, "We've built cities that can think."

Below, a billboard changed images automatically, showing the slogan of the Gateway campaign: *Invent Here. Stay Here. Belong Here.*

It was less a marketing line than a manifesto.

Ideas rarely stop at borders. As prototypes matured into policies, foreign delegations began to arrive — quiet observers from Seoul, Helsinki, Kigali,

Dubai. What started as Canada's experiment was becoming the world's inspiration. Innovation, it seemed, was its own language, and Canada was finally fluent enough to speak it abroad.

When a nation governs well, it begins to lead beyond its borders.

15

GATEWAY DIPLOMACY

The conference room in Geneva overlooked Lac Léman, its glass walls catching the reflection of both the Alps and the ambitions of the nations gathered within. Flags lined the circular table, their colours bright against the pale wood. The agenda read, *"Sustainable Industrial Zones and Global Investment Mobility."* It was the kind of session where speeches were usually polite and progress optional — but this time, something was different.

When Arjun spoke, he didn't begin with numbers or policy. He began with a story. "A few years ago," he said, "I stood on a patch of frozen land in northern Ontario. Nothing grew there — no trees, no jobs, no plans. Today, that same land powers factories, houses families, and trains engineers from forty countries. It didn't happen because we had capital. It happened because we had conviction."

He paused, letting the silence settle. "The Canada Global Gateway Zones are not special economic zones. They are shared economic futures. They prove that inclusion can be infrastructure and that capitalism can remember its conscience."

The room fell quiet, the kind of quiet that follows truth. When he finished, applause broke through like light through fog. Diplomacy, at least for a moment, had rediscovered sincerity.

The Gateway experiment had changed how Canada spoke to the world. Its cities became the country's ambassadors — living exhibits of what responsible globalization could look like. Foreign dignitaries toured them with curiosity: ministers from Indonesia studying renewable grids; African finance officials examining lease-based investment models; European mayors exploring digital governance. By the time they left, curiosity had turned into collaboration. The world, weary of speeches, was responding to something it could finally see.

Fifteen countries soon signed formal partnership agreements with Canada — mutual frameworks for knowledge exchange, student mobility, and shared innovation infrastructure.

Canada's approach to trade transformed as well. Traditional agreements had been transactional — tariffs, quotas, and footnotes of compromise. The Gateway Compact proposed something deeper: growth as a moral contract. Nations that joined committed to transparent taxation, 20 percent local employment in foreign projects, and net-zero GHG compliance by 2040. Economic exchange now came with a conscience attached. Evelyn summarized it best: "We used to compete on cost. Now we compete on character."

For Canada, diplomacy began closest to home. The tightening of H-1B visa programs in the United States had left tens of thousands of skilled professionals stranded in limbo. Canada seized the opportunity. The Gateway-North Initiative offered American companies a pragmatic lifeline — relocate R&D operations to Canadian Gateway Cities, retain your workforce, and enjoy tax predictability under a bilateral innovation accord. Within a few years, several major U.S. firms quietly shifted north. Silicon Valley media started calling Toronto, Halifax, and Calgary the "Arc of Opportunity." Arjun would later joke, "We didn't steal jobs from America — we rescued their dreams from their paperwork."

Beyond North America, the Gateway's reach expanded across the Indo-Pacific. India, Indonesia, Vietnam, and South Korea became active collaborators under the Pacific Bridge Program — an initiative that linked

Canada's Gateway Zones with Asia's technology and manufacturing corridors. Joint innovation hubs were established, one of them in Hyderabad, designed on the same principles of sustainability and co-governance. When Arjun addressed the opening ceremony there, he spoke with conviction: "Singapore showed discipline. Dubai showed speed. India shows scale. Canada offers stability. Together, we can design the century." The quote became a headline across India's newspapers. Canada, for once, was not a supporting actor in a global story — it was the protagonist.

Africa followed soon after. In Nairobi, the Pan-African Gateway Network was launched, bringing together Canadian technical expertise and African youth innovation. Together, they built solar villages, sustainable housing, and clean manufacturing. Instead of aid, Canada offered architecture — legal frameworks, financing models, and skills transfer. Evelyn put it simply: "We don't send cheques. We share blueprints." The statement resonated far beyond the continent.

Europe, too, recognized the potential. With the European Union pursuing its Green Industrial Plan, Canada's Gateway model became a natural ally. Through the Trans-Atlantic Green Alliance, both sides synchronized carbon markets and environmental reporting standards. For the first time, compliance and competitiveness aligned. A German delegate smiled during one summit and said, "You Canadians are exporting ethics again — and this time, we're buying."

From the Middle East came the next wave. Sovereign wealth funds from the United Arab Emirates and Saudi Arabia co-financed Gateway infrastructure projects — transit, ports, and data hubs — under strict sustainability covenants. In return, Canadian firms gained long-term contracts for green construction and hydrogen systems in the Gulf. These partnerships were no longer buyer-seller relationships, they were builder-builder alliances. When a journalist asked how Canada had managed to attract such investment without losing sovereignty, Arjun's answer was simple: "Because we entered not as a resource supplier, but as a resourceful partner."

Diplomacy, at its core, is about resonance — and the Gateway had given Canada a new tone. Its principles of transparency, inclusion, and shared stewardship became reference points in international negotiations. Think tanks in Washington, Paris, and Tokyo began referring to the *Gateway Doctrine*: sovereignty and cooperation can coexist when grounded in shared purpose.

The Gateway Cities hosted annual World Innovation Festivals, blending art, policy, and technology into celebrations of plural progress. Foreign delegations found themselves not in conferences but in communities. Slowly, the word *Canada* began to mean something larger — it was no longer just a peaceful country, but a courageous one, quietly redrawing the map of global cooperation.

Technology became diplomacy's new currency. Canada launched the Digital Silk Road, a secure, carbon-neutral data corridor linking Gateway Cities to their global partners. Powered entirely by renewable energy, it offered a model of transparent connectivity — a moral alternative to the debt-laden megaprojects that dominated the previous decade. The slogan read simply: *Bandwidth is the new diplomacy.*

Evelyn's speech at the World Economic Forum crystalized the idea. "A market can be both moral and modern," she said. "Profit without purpose is extraction. Purpose without profit is aspiration. Combine them, and you get endurance." The line made front pages from Zurich to Singapore. Even skeptical financiers began quoting her. Within months, a new global index emerged — measuring nations not just by GDP but by *Ethical Competitiveness*. Canada ranked first. The *Financial Times* called it "the rise of conscious capitalism, led from the North."

Traditional diplomacy began to evolve with the times. Ambassadors were joined — and sometimes replaced — by Gateway Envoys: scientists, technologists, Indigenous leaders, and entrepreneurs who spoke the universal language of collaboration. They represented Canada not through protocol, but through partnership. As Arjun often said, "Our ambassadors carry algorithms instead of briefcases." It was less a metaphor than a manifesto.

The Gateway Network also reshaped Canada's humanitarian presence. During disasters, its cities served as rapid-response hubs — dispatching clean-energy units, modular housing, and medical drones within hours. When a hurricane struck the Caribbean, Gateway crews arrived quietly and stayed long after the headlines faded. A local newspaper wrote, "Canada came without cameras — and left behind power." It was soft power at its most effective.

As the network expanded, a new identity began to form: the *Gateway Citizen* — builders, engineers, artists, and educators whose loyalty was defined not by borders but by belonging. A software developer from Lagos could hold Canadian residency while working on solar projects in Kenya under the same Gateway partnership framework. It was globalization without exploitation, mobility without displacement. Evelyn described it best: "We've moved from brain drain to brain circulation."

In 2038, the United Nations General Assembly passed a resolution recognizing the Gateway model as a global benchmark for equitable development. Canada received the Global Governance Award for Sustainable Innovation. Arjun, accepting it in New York, spoke quietly but firmly: "This honour belongs not to us, but to the idea that kindness can be competitive, and that fairness can scale." The applause that followed was both respectful and sustained.

Later that night, Evelyn stood on the terrace of the Canadian Mission in Geneva, watching the lake shimmer with the reflections of embassy lights. "Do you realize what we've done?" she asked. Arjun smiled. "We turned diplomacy into architecture."

Below them, the lake mirrored the lights of dozens of nations, but one emblem stood out — the Gateway symbol, a circle of interlocking paths. For centuries, countries had built walls to secure their futures. Canada, at last, had built doors.

Trade missions and treaties could fill headlines, but the real story was still human. Beneath the flags and frameworks lay the people carrying this new compact — the workers, teachers, migrants, and mayors who turned policy into pulse. Diplomacy may connect nations; empathy connects generations. The next chapter would return to the frontier within us.

The systems are built; now the story turns back to the soul.

16

THE HUMAN FRONTIER

The first snow of the season came quietly, the kind that softens sound and slows time. In the main square of Gateway City One, a child chased flakes that glowed under the lamplight. Around her, the buildings shimmered with faint heat from their solar façades. The scent of roasted coffee and cedar filled the air. A bus glided past without a sound, its electric hum lost beneath the laughter of the crowd.

Evelyn paused at the edge of the plaza, watching families emerge from shops and cafes, languages intertwining like wind currents. It struck her then — this was not a city built by engineers alone. It was built by intention, by trust, by people who had decided that coexistence could be a national project.

For generations, Canada's story had been about endurance: a vast land, a harsh climate, a quiet determination. The Gateway Cities added a new chapter — one about creation. They were not settlements carved out of wilderness; they were futures cultivated from collaboration. Every brick, every tree, every data line told the same story: *We built this together, and it worked.*

Life inside the Gateways blurred the boundaries between work, learning, and living. The average commute was under ten minutes, but the distance between opportunity and belonging had shrunk to zero. People no longer asked, "Where are you from?" but rather, "What are you building?" It was a subtle linguistic shift, yet it changed everything.

Public squares doubled as classrooms; research labs shared space with day-care centres; parks became meeting grounds for freelancers, poets, and programmers. On weekends, the air buzzed with outdoor markets — Ethiopian coffee beside Ukrainian pastries, Vietnamese pho beside bannock and maple candy. Cultures didn't compete; they converged.

Arjun liked to say that in Gateway Cities, "Diversity isn't a slogan — it's an economy."

The social contract here was tangible. Everyone contributed, and everyone could see the results. Taxes were visible, wages fair, and community projects voted on directly. Instead of bureaucracy, there was feedback. Instead of cynicism, transparency. When something broke, it was fixed not by complaint but by consensus.

At night, streetlights dimmed automatically to conserve energy. Solar panels tracked the moonlight as though unwilling to rest. The city seemed to breathe — a living organism sustained by trust and technology.

The Gateway Citizenship Program had become a global model. Newcomers arrived not as dependents but as contributors from day one. They paid taxes, built homes, joined local councils, and taught their languages in weekend schools. Many had fled bureaucratic stagnation elsewhere; here, they found momentum.

Each citizen signed the Covenant of Belonging upon arrival, a single-page document written in plain language: *To live here is to build here. To earn here is to give here. To belong here is to care here.*

It wasn't legally binding — but morally, it was unbreakable. In a country searching for its next chapter, belonging became the first principle.

In one neighbourhood, a Syrian architect taught carpentry to Indigenous youth, while an Anishinaabe elder taught the architect how to read the forest before cutting a single tree. Down the street, a Filipino nurse mentored a Canadian student in home-based elder care. A Ghanaian engineer ran a robotics club at the local school, where his students' first prototype — a waste-sorting robot — won a regional award. Each of these stories was small on its own, but together, they formed the heartbeat of the human frontier.

Arjun spent his weekends visiting communities — not as a bureaucrat but as a listener. At one community forum, a man in his fifties stood up and said, "I used to think I was too old to start over. Then I moved here. Now I run a solar installation company with my son. We employ twenty people. I'm not starting over — I'm continuing forward."

Moments like that convinced Arjun that policy could be personal. The Gateway model had turned governance into daily life — a quiet revolution measured in dignity instead of declarations.

Children growing up in these cities developed what sociologists called *plural fluency*: the ability to move between cultures without friction. Their classrooms had no majority language. Students switched from English to Cree to Mandarin with the ease of play. One teacher described them as "citizens of empathy."

Even civic rituals evolved. On Canada Day, fireworks were replaced by synchronized drone displays powered by renewable energy. The night sky filled with maple leaves, migrating birds, and digital auroras. Each display ended with a single line across the sky: *Home is what we build together*.

Not everything was perfect. There were still debates — about immigration quotas, housing prices, and cultural adaptation. Some critics called the cities "idealistic bubbles." But idealism, Evelyn reminded her team, was a foundation — not a flaw.

"The difference," she said during a council meeting, "is that when problems arise here, people stay to solve them. They don't leave blaming the system — they *are* the system."

Even conflicts were productive. Every argument, every protest, every policy revision added another layer of maturity to the experiment.

Social scientists began to notice something extraordinary. The Gateway citizens exhibited higher trust indices, lower anxiety levels, and stronger civic participation than the national average. They described themselves not as taxpayers or residents, but as *builders*.

A study by the University of British Columbia coined the phrase "Civic Belonging Index" to measure emotional investment in governance. Gateway Cities scored the highest in the world. It turned out that when people could see their fingerprints on their city, they treated it like something precious.

The Gateway model even redefined success. The richest residents weren't the ones with the largest homes but those whose names appeared most often in community acknowledgments. Social media, once a space for outrage, became a public ledger of gratitude. The city's communication app allowed residents to thank each other publicly for contributions big or small. Thousands of notes appeared daily — thanks for volunteering, for fixing a bike rack, for mentoring a student. It was the digital version of neighbourliness.

Evelyn joked that Canada had invented a new metric: Gross National Kindness.

One evening, Arjun walked through the Commons Garden — a long green corridor that wound through the city like a vein of calm. Children played under lamps powered by their own footsteps. In the distance, the sound of a violin mixed with wind. He stopped to speak with an elderly woman sitting on a bench. She was from Poland, he learned, and had lived through two migrations. "This place," she said softly, "feels like the Canada I imagined when I was young. A place that keeps its promises." For Arjun, that was the highest compliment any city could receive.

The concept of citizenship itself began to evolve. People identified less by nation and more by participation. When Gateway residents travelled abroad, they introduced themselves not by where they were from, but by what they represented. *"I'm from Gateway,"* they'd say, and the world began to understand what that meant — open minds, fair systems, and the quiet pride of progress made visible.

When the first group of Gateway citizens voted in a federal election, turnout reached nearly 100 percent. It wasn't obligation — it was enthusiasm. They weren't voting for change; they were voting to protect a model that worked.

As the city grew, its rhythm became Canada's rhythm — a blending of newness and nostalgia, of ancient stewardship and modern design. The

Gateway had begun as an experiment in economics. It had become an experiment in empathy.

Evelyn once told a journalist, "We thought we were building cities. What we built was belonging."

Years later, Arjun would add, "We wanted to make the frontier safe for investment. What we did was make it safe for dreams."

On the eve of the tenth anniversary of the first Gateway City, the country paused to celebrate. Across the network, lights dimmed for one minute. Then, as the clock struck nine, every rooftop, every streetlamp, and every drone lit up simultaneously in a synchronized burst of illumination that could be seen from space.

The prime minister addressed the nation: "We are no longer defined by what we extract from the Earth, but by what we create from imagination. Canada is not finished — it is beginning again."

In the plaza below, people looked up at the sky. Some cried. Others simply stood in silence, letting the light wash over them. For the first time in decades, hope felt organized.

Every movement finds its inheritors. As the first cohort of Gateway graduates, builders, and entrepreneurs came of age, they carried neither nostalgia nor cynicism — only expectation. They were raised in a Canada that built as it believed. The next pages belong to them: the generation that treats purpose as ordinary and progress as instinct.

Every policy writes its legacy in people.

PART III

THE FIRST FRONTIER: SUDBURY AND THE WEST

17

THE GATEWAY GENERATION

The school bell in Gateway City One didn't ring. It pulsed. A soft chime rippled through the campus, and students emerged from classrooms that opened directly into gardens. Wind turbines whispered above the rooftops, their slow rotations marking time more gently than clocks ever could.

In a classroom overlooking the river, a group of twelve-year-olds huddled around a digital globe. A boy from Edmonton and a girl from Nairobi zoomed in on a 3D map of Mars. "Terraforming algorithms," their teacher explained. "We're studying how planetary systems can teach us sustainable planning here on Earth."

At the back of the room, a holographic projection displayed the names of their group mentors — scientists from Toronto, Singapore, and Oslo — each volunteering an hour a week through the Gateway Learning Cloud. Geography had become collaboration — not distance.

These were the children of the Gateway Generation — born into a Canada that finally practised the inclusiveness it had long preached.

Their world was one of integration rather than instruction. Instead of memorizing facts, they built solutions. Every classroom had a Creation Table — a place where students designed, debated, and tested real projects. Lessons in math were taught through renewable energy models; history came alive through digital storytelling about Indigenous and immigrant experiences; ethics was not a subject but a habit.

At lunch, menus rotated weekly between global cuisines. One day bannock with lentil stew, another sushi beside pierogi. Every meal card carried a quote from a different culture: *"You learn a country through its kitchen."*

Teachers were guides — not gatekeepers. The curriculum flowed like a river — interdisciplinary, dynamic, and personal.

The Gateway Education Charter, adopted nationally by 2035, defined learning as *a public right and a shared responsibility.* Universities and vocational schools collaborated seamlessly, allowing young people to move between academic and applied programs without stigma. A coder could learn carpentry; an artist could study physics.

One student, fourteen-year-old Amira Chen, designed an AI model that optimized street lighting for migratory birds. Another, Tariq Whitecloud, used drone mapping to protect beaver habitats on Indigenous-managed land. Their projects were integrated into the city's planning database — real ideas shaping real outcomes.

When interviewed by a journalist, Tariq shrugged and said, "We don't do homework for school. We do homework for the city." The line became a national slogan.

The Gateway Generation grew up fluent in both technology and empathy. They were digital natives but emotional polyglots — able to read algorithms and emotions with equal fluency. Studies showed record levels of civic engagement among youth. Ninety-eight percent volunteered annually. Half of all teenagers participated in city governance simulations.

At sixteen, every student undertook a Civic Year — a paid mentorship in public service, research, or community entrepreneurship. The program was not symbolic; it was constitutional. It taught them that citizenship was a verb.

Arjun once said, "We used to prepare students for jobs that didn't exist. Now we prepare them to invent the ones that should."

Technology was everywhere, but never intrusive. AI tutors adjusted lessons in real time; virtual labs let students conduct chemical experiments without risk. Even so, analog skills were prized. Every child learned to plant, cook, repair, and write by hand. The Gateway philosophy held that sustainability began not with data but with dignity.

Evelyn described it this way: "A smart city isn't one that thinks for you. It's one that helps you think for yourself."

Cultural education became a mirror instead of a museum. Indigenous knowledge, once confined to elective courses, now anchored the entire curriculum. Students studied Cree geometry, Anishinaabe governance, and the Seven Grandfather Teachings alongside algebra and world history.

Each year ended with the Festival of Continuity, where students showcased projects blending tradition and innovation: 3D-printed canoes, coded beadwork patterns, renewable energy teepees. The festival wasn't about nostalgia — it was about narrative continuity, proof that heritage could evolve without disappearing.

When asked what made the Gateway Generation different, their principal replied, "They don't ask whether something is Indigenous or immigrant. They ask whether it's interesting."

THE SEVEN GRANDFATHER TEACHINGS

Originating from the Anishinaabe people, the Seven Grandfather Teachings embody a holistic philosophy of how to live in harmony with oneself, others, and the land. They are:

1. **Wisdom (Nibwaakaawin):** To cherish knowledge and use it for the good of all.
2. **Love (Zaagi'idiwin):** To know peace is to know love; love must be unconditional.
3. **Respect (Minaadendamowin):** To honour all creation and value the balance in relationships.
4. **Bravery (Aakode'ewin):** To face life with courage and integrity, doing what is right even when it is difficult.
5. **Honesty (Gwayakwaadiziwin):** To live truthfully with self and others.
6. **Humility (Dabaadendiziwin):** To know oneself as a sacred part of creation; equality with all beings.
7. **Truth (Debwewin):** To understand and speak the truth, living all these teachings fully.

Family life evolved too. In Gateway Cities, education extended beyond schools. Parents attended Learning Circles, where they exchanged skills — gardening, accounting, language, coding. Grandparents taught oral history workshops, ensuring cultural memory kept pace with innovation.

Sociologists noticed a striking outcome: loneliness declined. Intergenerational bonds, once weakened by urban isolation, re-emerged as a civic feature. Integrated childcare centres had become community anchors, places where parents met, teachers collaborated, and children moved seamlessly between care and learning. What began as social design matured into a quiet engine of belonging. Even apartment buildings incorporated communal kitchens and play spaces. The architecture itself seemed to say, *You belong here.*

At the national level, the Gateway Generation began reshaping politics. Many turned eighteen with a deep distrust of polarization and a preference for participatory governance. They formed digital assemblies where citizens could debate bills in plain language. When the first of them ran for federal office, their campaign slogan read simply: *Less talk. More doing.*

They had no patience for cynicism. For them, government wasn't an institution; it was a tool. And like any tool, it should evolve — or be redesigned.

By 2040, the first full cohort of Gateway graduates entered the workforce. Some became climate scientists, others urban planners, artists, or teachers. Many returned to their home countries to build similar models. The diaspora of innovation Canada had once feared was now an asset — a network of goodwill extending across the globe.

An observer at the United Nations noted, "You can always tell a Gateway graduate. They listen first."

Listening had become the new form of leadership.

Not everyone outside the cities understood the change. Critics argued that the Gateway Generation lived in a bubble of privilege, detached from the struggles of rural and traditional communities. Evelyn countered, "It's not a bubble. It's a blueprint."

To address the concern, the federal government launched the Gateway Outreach Program, sending youth ambassadors to support education reform in remote and Indigenous regions. The movement spread organically; within five years, 90 percent of Canadian municipalities had adopted at least one Gateway education principle.

The model proved contagious because it was generous.

Culturally, the Gateway Generation carried an ease that their parents envied. They wore mixed identities with pride — Punjabi-Canadian-Quebecois, Nigerian-Inuit, Polish-Filipino. They weren't hyphenated; they were harmonized.

Their music blended throat singing with lo-fi beats; their art mixed beadwork with augmented reality. Their slang drew from five languages and one shared sense of humour. When foreign visitors asked, "Where are you from?" they answered, "From the future."

And they meant it.

Arjun, now older and more reflective, often walked through the campus gardens at dusk, watching the next generation move with confidence he had only dreamed of at their age. "They have no memory of borders," he said once to Evelyn. "Only networks."

She smiled. "That's what happens when belonging is inherited instead of earned."

He nodded, gazing at the skyline. "Then perhaps we've done our job. We've made hope hereditary."

In the plaza below, the students of Gateway University prepared for graduation. The ceremony was outdoors, under a canopy of light. Instead of a stage, there was a circle. Elders, teachers, and students sat side by side, symbolizing equality in purpose.

As the anthem played — its verses alternating between English, French, and Cree — a thousand drones lifted into the night sky, forming a luminous maple leaf surrounded by smaller stars. The crowd cheered, not for spectacle, but for symbolism: Canada had finally learned to shine together.

Evelyn took the podium, her voice steady and proud. "You," she told the graduates, "are not inheriting the world as it is. You're inheriting the tools to rebuild it as it should be. You are not the next generation. You are the continuation."

The applause that followed wasn't loud but it was lasting.

Later that night, Arjun walked home through quiet streets lit by soft amber light. The air smelled of rain and pine. Somewhere nearby, music played — an old folk song remixed with electronic rhythm. He stopped, listening. It was the sound of the old and the new keeping time together.

He thought about how far the country had come — from hesitation to conviction, from frontier to future. For the first time in years, he felt certain that the idea they had dreamed in a Tim Hortons cafe so long ago had truly taken root.

Above him, the city pulsed with light — each rooftop, each window, each mind alive with possibility. Canada, once cautious, had learned to imagine boldly again.

And in that glow, Arjun realized that the human frontier had never been about space or distance. It had always been about spirit.

What one generation builds, the next must balance. The Gateway experiment now faced the slow arithmetic of endurance — how to convert momentum into maturity, and idealism into inheritance. It was time to count not the cranes, but the consequences.

Momentum matures into measurement.

18

THE ECONOMIC LEGACY

The sound of construction had changed. Where once the clang of steel and hum of machines filled the air, now it was subtler — the whirr of drones planting trees along a new solar highway, the low hum of delivery bots gliding through quiet streets. The Gateway Cities had moved from building themselves to maintaining themselves, their growth no longer a rush of momentum but a rhythm of maturity.

Arjun stood at the balcony of the National Gateway Council, overlooking the skyline that had once been a dream on paper. Wind turbines turned slowly beyond the horizon. Freight pods traced thin blue lines of light along the elevated tracks. Somewhere below, a bus stopped silently, its door opening to a group of schoolchildren carrying robotics kits and violin cases.

He smiled faintly. *This is what legacy sounds like*, he thought. Not applause, not noise — just continuity.

By the late 2040s, the Gateway Network had become the backbone of the Canadian economy. Together, the cities accounted for nearly a quarter of national GDP, while occupying less than 2 percent of its land. Exports were no longer dominated by commodities but by code, clean energy systems, and creative services. The trade surplus grew steadily, but more impressive was the *social surplus* — trust, participation, and public well-being.

A report from the World Economic Forum called it "the most stable model of adaptive capitalism on Earth." *The Economist* described it more succinctly: "Canada has made sustainability lucrative."

The foundation of that prosperity lay in the Gateway Continuum Model, a self-reinforcing economic loop that replaced extraction with regeneration. Every dollar spent inside a Gateway City circulated, on average, 2.7 times before leaving — through wages, leases, reinvestments, and civic projects. Taxes flowed not into distant bureaucracies but back into visible improvements.

The Gateway Dividend — a modest quarterly payout funded by collective lease profits — provided every citizen with an annual share of the city's success. It wasn't charity; it was acknowledgment. A nurse in Halifax, a coder in Edmonton, a teacher in Saskatoon — all received their portion of the shared prosperity they helped create. The dividend symbolized the shift from a government of redistribution to an economy of participation.

Evelyn called it "capitalism with a conscience and a memory."

Under the leadership of the Gateway Generation, finance itself had evolved. Traditional banks transformed into Ethical Capital Networks, where investment decisions were weighted not only by profit but by purpose. Metrics like carbon offset yield, community uplift, and knowledge equity became as vital as return on investment.

One of the brightest of the new generation, Amira Chen — once the student who had built an AI for migratory lighting systems — now led the Global Stewardship Fund, an institution dedicated to financing sustainable development projects across the world. Her model drew on the same principles she had grown up with in Gateway schools: transparency, fairness, and long-term responsibility.

When asked what guided her, she quoted a familiar line: "We don't build to win. We build to last."

Canada's national budget began to reflect the Gateway philosophy. Rather than funding departments, it funded *outcomes*. Ministries were restructured into Mission Portfolios: Clean Energy, Human Development,

Ethical Trade, Cultural Resilience. The bureaucracy shrank even as effectiveness grew.

Public officials were evaluated not by compliance but by contribution. Civic data dashboards showed progress in real time — poverty reduction, carbon intensity, innovation metrics, and citizen satisfaction. Governance had finally become as agile as the private sector.

A senior journalist observed, "Canada stopped trying to manage society and started curating it."

At the community level, small businesses thrived under the Micro-Equity Program, a system that allowed residents to own fractional shares in local enterprises. When a bakery succeeded, every neighbour who invested a small amount in its early days earned dividends. This quiet network of ownership blurred the lines between entrepreneur and citizen.

"Ownership," Arjun often said, "is the most powerful form of inclusion."

The same logic extended to housing. Leased land ensured affordability, but ownership of *community equity* gave everyone a stake in the city's success. People didn't speculate on property values — they invested in stability.

As the economy matured, the question shifted from *growth* to *grace*. Could prosperity remain humble? Could it sustain meaning?

The Gateway Generation answered through design. Luxury developments were banned; instead, wealth expressed itself through contribution — foundations, research fellowships, and social enterprises. The richest citizens competed to build the most impactful projects — not the tallest towers.

In one city, a group of entrepreneurs funded a *Quiet Zone*, a vast urban forest for reflection and recreation. In another, a retired engineer built a mentorship academy for trades apprentices. Status had been redefined: success measured by how many futures you financed.

The international community took notice. Global capital began flowing to Canada not because of low taxes but because of *low risk*. Stability had become the new luxury. Investors trusted a system that rewarded honesty and punished opacity.

At the annual World Bank Summit, a former critic of the Gateway model admitted, "Canada has done what we all feared impossible: created a high-trust society that's also high-performance."

Evelyn, now serving as Canada's first Chief Steward of the Economy, often reflected on how far they had come. During a quiet interview with a journalist, she said, "In the beginning, we were just trying to fix a few broken systems. We didn't know we were designing a civilization upgrade."

When asked about her legacy, she smiled. "Legacy isn't what you leave behind. It's what continues without you."

Arjun spent more time teaching than governing. His lectures at Gateway University drew crowds from across the world. Students quoted him the way earlier generations had quoted Carney or Diefenbaker. Yet he carried himself with humility. He began each lecture the same way: "The first lesson of leadership is to remember who's missing from the table."

One afternoon, during a discussion on the evolution of capitalism, a student asked him if he thought the Gateway model would last forever. Arjun paused, then said, "Nothing human is forever. But decency tends to outlive cynicism."

The class went silent. Then they applauded.

In 2050, the Canadian Centennial of Innovation marked the ten-year anniversary of the Gateway Charter. The event drew leaders from seventy nations to Ottawa. On Parliament Hill, holographic panels displayed live data from every Gateway City: air quality, education indices, public health, and employment metrics — all in the green.

The prime minister, herself a Gateway Generation graduate, addressed the crowd: "Once, we measured success by what we could extract from the Earth. Now we measure it by what we can return to it. Canada has become not the richest nation, but perhaps the most balanced."

As she spoke, the crowd held up their phones, projecting thousands of small lights into the evening — a constellation of shared pride.

The transformation wasn't just national — it was philosophical. The concept of *work* itself had evolved. Automation and AI had taken over repetitive tasks, but instead of displacing workers, the Gateway system had retrained them into fields of creativity, care, and community management. The average Canadian worked fewer hours but contributed more meaningfully. Productivity was measured not in output but in *impact*.

The result was a quieter, happier society. People again had time — for art, for family, for conversation. Time had become the new wealth.

Economists around the world debated how to replicate Canada's success. Some said it was geography, others governance. But the truth was simpler. The system worked because it was human.

Gateway Cities had never been perfect, but they were honest. They built trust not by avoiding mistakes but by admitting them. That transparency — raw, unpolished, and real — became their most valuable export.

On the final day of the Centennial, Arjun and Evelyn stood together at the Ottawa River promenade, the same stretch where, years before, they had first spoken about possibility over a pair of steaming Tim Hortons cups. Snow drifted across the water, and the Parliament dome glowed softly in the distance.

Evelyn turned to him. "Do you think they'll remember us?"

Arjun chuckled. "If we've done this right, they won't have to."

They stood in silence, watching as the city lights reflected across the river — bright, steady, and shared. Somewhere in those reflections, two lives of service dissolved gently into the collective glow of a nation that had learned to build, to belong, and to believe.

By now, the question had reversed itself. The world that once asked, *Can Canada change?* began asking, *How did it do it?* The quiet country had become a case study. To share its method was not boast, but responsibility. The next step would translate legacy into language — a blueprint the world could read.

Canada, once student, now becomes teacher.

19

THE GLOBAL BLUEPRINT

The world had been watching quietly. For decades, international summits had been filled with talk of innovation, inclusion, and sustainability, but progress had always seemed like a distant horizon — something admired more than achieved. Then, from the northern edge of the map, a small miracle unfolded.

The Gateway Model had taken root in Canada, but its branches reached far beyond. By 2055, replicas began sprouting in every corner of the planet — each with its own flavour, each adapted to its own soil, yet all nourished by the same principles: transparency, fairness, and courage.

No one called them "Canadian cities." They called them *Gateways* — not to imitate, but to belong to the same vision of possibility.

The first to adopt the framework was Kenya, whose Savannah Gateway Zone transformed dry grasslands outside Nairobi into a thriving clean-tech corridor. Powered entirely by solar energy and run by a coalition of local cooperatives, it became a case study in inclusive capitalism.

When a journalist asked its director what inspired the design, she replied simply: "We borrowed Canada's idea of belonging — and translated it into Swahili."

Within five years, East Africa's renewable sector became its largest employer, exporting green technologies across the continent. Aid dependency declined. The Gateway had taught not charity, but self-reliance.

In India, the state of Gujarat launched the G-Connect Smart Zone, a partnership between the Canadian Gateway Council and local entrepreneurs. It operated under the same 80/20 employment principle — 80 percent foreign specialists and 20 percent local workers — but soon the ratio reversed as Indian engineers rose through the ranks.

The zone's anchor institution, the Nehru-Carney Institute for Ethical Economics, became a magnet for policy thinkers from around the world. In its opening speech, the Indian prime minister remarked, "Canada gave us a blueprint, but we've written our own chapter."

For Arjun, who watched the ceremony from Ottawa, that was the dream fulfilled — not imitation, but inspiration.

Across Europe, the Gateway idea blended seamlessly with existing green frameworks. In Germany, the Rhein-Main ReGeneration Hub turned an abandoned industrial area into a climate-neutral manufacturing zone. France reimagined Marseille's port as a "Cultural Gateway," where artists, coders, and climate scientists shared the same funding pool.

The European Union soon integrated the Gateway Charter into its Green Deal legislation. Instead of competition, nations now traded sustainability metrics the way they once traded goods.

Evelyn joked in a speech at Davos, "We started a chain reaction — capitalism with a carbon conscience."

In the Middle East, the transformation was as symbolic as it was practical. The Dubai Renewal Corridor, co-designed with Canadian engineers, replaced oil storage facilities with hydrogen plants, vertical farms, and desalination research centres. Saudi Arabia's NEOM project — once criticized as futuristic excess — restructured itself under the Gateway Compact, embedding environmental and human rights audits into every contract.

Even regional rivals found common ground. Shared water grids and renewable energy pipelines replaced political boundaries with practical cooperation.

When reporters asked a Gulf minister what caused this unlikely partnership, he smiled: "We learned that sunlight doesn't stop for borders."

In Southeast Asia, where dense populations and rising seas had long challenged sustainability, the Gateway model proved revolutionary. Indonesia's Archipelago Nexus integrated renewable micro-grids across seven hundred islands, linking remote fishing villages into a shared digital economy. Vietnam's Delta Gate became a world leader in sustainable aquaculture. Singapore established the Lee Kuan Yew-Evelyn Grant Fellowship to train policymakers in ethical governance and urban resilience.

At the fellowship's first graduation, a young woman from Manila summed it up: "Singapore taught us how to grow up fast. Canada taught us how to stay kind."

The Americas were slower to adopt — until success became too visible to ignore. In the United States, California and Washington state implemented *Gateway-lite* programs, creating renewable tech clusters inspired by the Canadian framework. Silicon Valley investors began referring to "northern principles" — decentralization, co-ownership, and ethics-first design — as competitive advantages.

Mexico launched Zona Puente Verde, a manufacturing corridor that linked directly with Gateway supply chains through blockchain trade protocols. Within three years, cross-border logistics cut emissions by 60 percent and corruption by even more.

By 2058, the North American continent operated less like three separate economies and more like one transparent ecosystem.

The Digital Silk Road, once just a Canadian-led experiment, evolved into the World Data Compact, a planetary cloud of shared, carbon-neutral data centres. Every participating nation contributed encrypted environmental, health, and education data for collaborative research. AI models trained across continents began solving problems no single country could: curing rare diseases, predicting droughts, designing fairer tax systems.

The project's founding document quoted the original Gateway Charter: *Knowledge, like air, must circulate freely to sustain life.*

For the first time in history, global cooperation was not idealism — it was infrastructure.

At the United Nations, a new institution emerged: the Global Council for Regenerative Economies (GCRE). Headquartered in Vancouver, it served as both think tank and tribunal, ensuring Gateway-aligned cities worldwide adhered to environmental and ethical benchmarks.

Unlike previous bodies burdened by bureaucracy, the Council operated with radical transparency. All deliberations were live-streamed; decisions were data-verified. Citizens, not governments, held the right to petition for review.

The Council's emblem — an infinity loop encircling a maple leaf — became as recognizable as the UN flag itself.

By 2060, one-third of the world's GDP flowed through some form of Gateway-inspired governance. Extreme poverty declined. Carbon emissions fell faster than predicted by any Paris Agreement model. Education access expanded through digital cross-border networks. The line between "developed" and "developing" nations began to fade.

Economists called it *The Great Convergence.*

But Arjun, invited to address the World Assembly in Geneva, called it something simpler. "Human progress," he said, "isn't the rise of one country — it's the lifting of everyone's floor."

He spoke without notes, his voice steady yet full of wonder. "We began with the hope that Canada could learn from the world. We ended with the world learning from Canada. But what truly matters is that we've all learned from each other."

The hall erupted in applause. Some delegates stood; others simply bowed their heads in quiet respect. It was a moment when diplomacy sounded like gratitude.

In the years that followed, Canada's role evolved from leader to mentor. Every Gateway City was paired with a *twin zone* abroad — Halifax with Nairobi, Edmonton with Hanoi, Vancouver with Marseille — exchanging students, entrepreneurs, and policymakers in a permanent rotation of learning.

A new generation of global citizens emerged: polyglot, purposeful, and practical. They were as comfortable quoting an Indigenous proverb as they were writing quantum code. Borders still existed, but they had lost their fear.

Evelyn, now retired from public office but still restless in purpose, became a visiting fellow at the Institute for Global Stewardship in Kyoto. During one panel, a moderator asked her whether she thought the Gateway movement had changed the world.

She smiled. "Change isn't a switch. It's a sequence. The world was ready — we just showed it a way to move."

After the session, students surrounded her, asking what Canada's secret had been. Her answer was as simple as it was profound: "We stopped apologizing for our decency and started building with it."

The moral architecture of global capitalism had shifted. Stock markets now included "trust indices" alongside earnings reports. Corporations competed on sustainability certifications. Cities published *Happiness Ledgers* as part of their financial disclosures.

For the first time in modern history, virtue had market value.

When Arjun spoke at the annual Values Forum, held that year in Cape Town, he reflected on this reversal. "History," he said, "was written by those who conquered. The future will be written by those who collaborate."

Behind him, the screen displayed a simple image: Earth, seen from orbit, crisscrossed by glowing lines connecting every Gateway on the planet — a constellation of cooperation.

The Gateway Generation, now in their thirties and forties, held seats in parliaments and presidencies. They led companies, universities, and think tanks across continents. Their governance style was distinct: pragmatic, kind, allergic to arrogance. They made mistakes — but they made them transparently.

One African president, a Gateway graduate herself, described her philosophy during an interview: "We learned from Canada that progress isn't about perfection. It's about persistence. It's about having the courage to fix what you build."

The shift wasn't universal. Some nations resisted, clinging to old hierarchies or exploiting loopholes in the Compact. But even in those places, the cultural tide had turned. Young people compared their governments to Gateway benchmarks. Citizens demanded fairness the way consumers once demanded Wi-Fi.

What began as an experiment in one snowy nation had become a moral baseline for civilization.

In Ottawa, now the symbolic capital of the Global Gateway Network, an archival exhibit displayed the original draft of the first proposal — Canadian Frontier Development Zones (CFDZ) — dated almost forty years earlier. The faded printout still bore coffee stains and margin notes.

Next to it stood a photograph: Arjun and Evelyn, younger, laughing outside a small Tim Hortons near Parliament Hill.

The caption read: "Where the future began — over coffee, conviction, and kindness."

That winter, at a private gathering of former Gateway leaders, Arjun stood quietly by a window as snow fell outside — a familiar, patient snow that seemed to connect past and present.

Evelyn approached, now slower in step but as sharp as ever. "Do you ever wonder," she asked, "what would have happened if we hadn't acted back then?"

He looked out at the glowing city beyond, lights reflecting on the river. "I think someone else would have," he said softly. "Because ideas like this aren't owned. They're inherited."

They stood together in silence, watching the lights of a world that no longer just lived side by side, but forward together.

Every revolution ends in reflection. As Frontier Nation took its place among the stories of how countries rise, Canada found itself in an unfamiliar role — leader by example, not by declaration. The world had noticed. Yet the truest victory was not global admiration but domestic awakening: the rediscovery of a courage that had always been there, waiting under the snow.

The map folds back into memory.

20

THE QUIET COUNTRY THAT LED THE WORLD

The river never forgot. On winter mornings, mist still rose from the Ottawa River, drifting like memory across the bridge. Parliament's dome stood unchanged, a familiar silhouette against the pale blue sky. And somewhere in the distance, a cafe still brewed coffee, its scent carrying faint echoes of the day an idea had quietly begun — the day two people looked at their country and saw not what it was, but what it could be.

It had been decades since that conversation at Tim Hortons, and yet, the essence of it lingered in every Gateway City, every solar-lit street, every voice that now spoke of Canada with renewed respect. A nation once known for its politeness had, without fanfare, become the architect of the world's most humane revolution.

Canada had not conquered, coerced, or claimed. It had *demonstrated.* It led by doing what came naturally — listening, including, and improving — until the world realized that quiet competence could be more transformative than loud ambition.

The world didn't notice it at first. Change rarely announces itself with noise. It seeps in gently, like spring through thawing ground. But when the first cities flourished, when the first foreign investors returned not for profit but for partnership, when nations began sending delegations not to lecture but to learn, that's when people began to understand.

Leadership could wear mittens.

Decades later, children born into the Gateway Generation knew this Canada not as an exception but as normal. They grew up seeing the maple leaf not just as a symbol of peace, but as a promise of possibility — proof that kindness and competence could coexist at scale.

They didn't marvel at the solar highways, the transparent governance apps, or the carbon-neutral cities. To them, these weren't miracles. They were maintenance — the upkeep of decency.

And that, perhaps, was the greatest legacy: goodness had become institutional.

Arjun visited the old cafe one last time. The chairs had changed, the décor had been updated, but the window still framed the same view — the frozen river, the passersby, the gentle rhythm of a country unhurried by its own greatness.

He sat with a cup of coffee — still a double-double, out of habit — and watched as two young people at the next table discussed a start-up idea for climate-positive construction materials. Their excitement was contagious, their language fluent in purpose and practicality.

They spoke about *impact metrics* and *open-source patents*, about *Indigenous design ethics* and *renewable grids*. They didn't realize it, but they were continuing a conversation that had started right there, many years before.

And Arjun, now older and slower, smiled. The idea no longer belonged to him — and that was the point.

Outside, the world had changed beyond recognition. Global cooperation was now as routine as trade once was. Wars had grown rare, replaced by competition for innovation rather than domination. Even in countries that had resisted the Gateway framework, young leaders had emerged who insisted on transparency and fairness as non-negotiable.

Humanity had learned something profound from the Canadian experiment: decency, scaled properly, could be an engine of growth.

It turned out that people didn't need perfection — they needed participation. They didn't crave wealth — they craved worth. And when a system provided both, civilization steadied itself.

Evelyn's name was etched on the wall of the Global Council for Regenerative Economies in Vancouver, just below Arjun's. Visitors often paused there, reading the inscription carved into the marble: *We believed that progress should feel like belonging.*

Schoolchildren recited those words during civic lessons. University students quoted them in commencement speeches. To most, they were history. To a few, they were instruction.

In a quiet neighbourhood in Mississauga, Arjun's home overlooked a park planted with young maple trees. The local community had renamed it Gateway Grove. Every spring, citizens gathered there to celebrate *Belonging Day*, a festival that honoured the city's founding principles.

They came with flags from every nation, food from every culture, and songs from every language. The event had no speeches, no politicians, no sponsors — just neighbours.

As evening approached, people lit lanterns and released them into the air. Each carried a single handwritten wish. One floated above Arjun's head and drifted away slowly, its flicker reflected in his glasses. It read: "Thank you for imagining us."

Years passed. The world moved on, as it must. New leaders rose; new technologies emerged. Gateway Cities evolved again, merging into *living networks* of distributed governance. The line between the physical and digital world blurred until cities were as much cloud as concrete.

But through every iteration, one truth held: progress without compassion was still regression. And Canada — that quiet, measured, occasionally underestimated country — remained the global conscience reminding everyone of it.

When historians later wrote about the twenty-first century, they called the movement "The Canadian Renaissance" — the era when empathy became infrastructure.

At a centennial symposium marking a hundred years since the founding of the first Gateway City, scholars and policymakers from around the world gathered in Ottawa. They filled the great hall of the National Gallery, now powered entirely by hydrogen fuel cells. A new generation of leaders — many of them children of immigrants, many of them from nations that once received Canada's mentorship — took the stage to share what the Gateway legacy meant to them.

One speaker, a young president from Kenya, said: "Canada taught us that greatness isn't about how many follow you — it's about how many you lift."

Another, an economist from Brazil, added: "History will say that Canada exported kindness — and it paid better than oil."

That evening, as dusk fell over the capital, the crowd gathered by the river once more. A thousand drones rose into the sky, tracing a lighted arc across the water. On the Parliament façade, a message appeared — not in English or French, but in the many languages of the world: *Home is what we build together.*

For a long moment, the crowd stood in silence. Some held hands. Others simply looked upward, their faces reflecting the golden light of a nation that had, at last, become what it had always wanted to be: an idea big enough for everyone.

Later that night, a documentary filmmaker closed his script with a simple narration: "Canada did not lead the world through conquest, nor through wealth, nor through force. It led by being the first to believe that fairness could be a strategy. And when the world finally followed, it discovered that fairness was also its future."

Long after the lights dimmed, the snow returned, soft as ever, quiet as truth. And along the banks of the Ottawa River, the wind whispered through the trees, carrying a voice that was less memory than message — the enduring sound of a country that once decided to lead not by being louder, but by being *better.*

And so the circle closes where it began — by the Ottawa River, or perhaps any river that runs through a nation learning to believe again. The story that started with a sketch and a cup of coffee ends with a simple conviction:

the possible is not a place; it's a practice. What matters now is who continues the drawing.

The story closes, but the invitation begins.

EPILOGUE

WHAT CANADA MUST ASK ITSELF NOW

The story of Arjun and the Gateway experiment ends there, but the story of Canada does not. What comes next depends on the questions we are finally willing to ask ourselves. There comes a moment in every nation's story when the quiet questions accumulate into a reckoning. Not a crisis, not a collapse — just a recognition that the path behind no longer matches the path ahead. Canada is standing in that moment now. And for the first time in a generation, the questions are no longer technical, or bureaucratic, or incremental. They are existential.

Who are we building this country for? What future are we preparing? And why, despite our abundance, do so many feel left behind?

For years we drifted on the assumption that stability was progress. That calm was competence. That our advantages — land, resources, diversity, safety, trust — were a permanent inheritance. But advantages are not permanent. They erode under complacency, under slow systems, under the belief that time is on our side.

The truth is simple: Canada has been living below its potential for decades, and the consequences have finally become impossible to ignore.

Housing is unaffordable. Newcomers arrive only to struggle. Cities buckle under pressure. Young families lose faith that home ownership will ever be within reach. Employers cannot find the talent they need. And despite being a nation rich in minerals, water, land, and stability, our economic growth lags behind similar countries.

This is not a shortage of capability. It is a shortage of courage — of design, of ambition, of willingness to build at scale and speed. Frontier Nation was written because the next era of Canada cannot be defined by drift. It must be defined by deliberate action. And that begins by asking the questions we have long avoided.

HAS CANADA KEPT ITS PROMISE TO IMMIGRANTS?

This is one of the most sensitive questions in our national conversation — and one of the most necessary. For decades, Canada has positioned itself as a beacon for newcomers seeking safety, stability, and opportunity. The message was consistent: *Come, build a life, contribute to a country that rewards effort and ambition.*

But ask many recent immigrants privately — and the answer is often quietly devastating. Highly educated professionals working survival jobs. Foreign-trained experts blocked by licensing barriers. Newcomers unable to find housing within a reasonable commute. International students trapped between expenses and exploitation.

Canada did not intend to deceive anyone. But intentions do not matter as much as outcomes. The promise of Canada — the real one, the one that generations believed in — was never about passports or paperwork. It was about possibility.

Today, many feel that possibility shrinking.

This does not mean immigration was a mistake. On the contrary — immigration is Canada's greatest asset, economically, socially, and morally. But we expanded our intake without expanding our capacity. Our immigration system grew vertically while our housing, transit, training, and regulatory systems stayed horizontal.

Immigrants did not fail Canada. Canada failed to prepare for immigrants.

Gateway Cities are designed to correct that imbalance: purpose-built places where newcomers can step directly into the economy, not wait years for their credentials to be recognized or compete in overcrowded markets. Cities where employers, training systems, and communities grow together — not in conflict, but in coordination.

For Canada to reclaim its credibility, it must build places worthy of the people it attracts.

WHY IS A RESOURCE-RICH NATION ONE OF THE HIGHEST-TAXED IN THE WORLD?

Ask Canadians what frustrates them most and you will hear a quiet resentment: Why do we pay so much tax and see so little transformation? Not because Canadians oppose taxes — most believe in collective responsibility. But they want efficiency, clarity, and visible results.

Right now, we have none of the three.

A country with this much water, land, energy, minerals, trust, and global reputation should not need to tax its citizens at among the highest effective rates in the OECD. High tax burdens are not inherently wrong — but they must produce prosperity, infrastructure, mobility, and innovation.

Instead, Canadians see decades-long project timelines, bottlenecked services, aging infrastructure, and slow-moving approvals. The issue is not how much we collect. It is how little we convert.

Gateway Cities introduce a new compact:

- Lower taxes for reinvestment — not extraction
- Corporate incentives tied to local hiring, training, and innovation
- Long-term leases that create revenue without selling land
- Fast, transparent regulatory pathways that reduce public cost instead of increasing it

Countries like Singapore — and, through targeted free-zone and sector-specific regimes, the UAE — grew not by lowering taxes for everyone, but by tying tax incentives to investment, reinvestment, and national development priorities. Canada can — and must — do the same.

If we want to protect the social contract, taxes must not feel like punishment. They must feel like participation.

THE QUESTION OF SAFETY — AND WHY OUR CITIES FEEL LIKE THEY'RE FRAYING?

There is one question Canadians whisper more than they discuss: *Why does it feel like our big cities are becoming less safe?*

It is a hard question, because it brushes against identity. Canada sees itself — proudly — as gentle, welcoming, orderly. But a country cannot solve what it refuses to name.

The truth is uncomfortable but clarifying: Canada's crime problem is not fundamentally a policing problem. It is a capacity problem. Crime rises where systems crack. And systems crack where a nation places more strain than its infrastructure can carry.

We have poured all our growth into four or five metropolitan zones — Toronto, Vancouver, Calgary, Edmonton, Winnipeg — and then wondered why transit systems buckle, shelters overflow, and urban cores struggle to absorb every form of pressure at once.

Cities are not breaking because they are failing. They are breaking because we have demanded they carry the entire weight of the Canadian dream by themselves. Crime follows congestion. Congestion follows bad planning. Bad planning follows political fear.

And fear has been governing our growth for twenty years.

The gateway model confronts this directly — not with slogans, but with physics. When you distribute population, you distribute pressure. When you distribute pressure, you reduce strain. And when you reduce strain, crime stops spiralling.

This is not theory; it is how cities worldwide protect themselves.

Singapore did it with planning. Finland with design. Sweden with zoning.

Safety is not a mystery. It is architecture. Canada is the rare country that has the land to do it but refuses to use it.

The question we must ask now is stark: "Why do we force every challenge into the same postcodes — and then punish those postcodes for collapsing?"

Gateway Cities answer that question by removing the structural conditions that enable crime to take root:

- Jobs match people. No long-term underemployment.
- Housing supply grows ahead of demand. Not twenty years late.
- Mixed-income zoning prevents poverty clusters.
- Transit is built for reliability and visibility.
- Mental-health centres and social services are designed into districts from day one.
- Predictive digital dashboards let communities see problems early.
- Indigenous co-governance embeds restorative justice from the foundation up.
- Freight and commuter flows are separated, preventing unsafe urban choke points.

Most crime prevention happens long before a uniform arrives.

It happens in the design of a street, the shape of a transit corridor, the ratio of jobs to residents, the availability of support systems, the decision to build ahead of population rather than behind it.

Gateway Cities offer something Canada has never tried: urban safety by design — not emergency response.

And perhaps the hardest question of all is the simplest: "How long will Canada accept rising crime as inevitable, when the real problem is that we keep forcing twenty-first-century pressures into twentieth-century maps?"

Crime is not an urban failure. It is a national one.

And one we can fix — but only by building where Canada has never built, distributing opportunity where Canada has never looked, and designing cities that absorb growth instead of breaking under it.

WHY CAN'T CANADIANS BUILD QUICKLY ANYMORE?

This may be the defining question of our decade. A country that built a transcontinental railway in six years now struggles to build transit lines in twenty. A nation that built highways, dams, energy corridors, and urban infrastructure at global pace now loses momentum in environmental reviews, court delays, and overlapping jurisdictions.

None of this is because Canadians lack skill or ambition. It is because our systems are designed for prevention — not production.

The Gateway model approaches this differently:

- Approvals in months — not years
- Single-window governance
- Digital-first permitting
- Transparent dashboards that show progress, delays, and emissions in real time
- Co-governance with Indigenous nations from day one — not afterthought consultation
- Canada does not need to compromise safety or environment to build faster. It needs to replace opacity with clarity.

The outdated idea that "slow equals safe" has cost us competitiveness, investment, and confidence. The new reality is that slow equals exclusion — because the longer a project takes, the fewer Canadians can afford the results.

WHAT INDUSTRIES WILL SUSTAIN CANADA IN THE NEXT FIFTY YEARS?

This is not a question of ideology but of survival. The world is reorganizing around new supply chains, new energy systems, new security alliances, and new technological frontiers. Canada cannot cling to yesterday's economic architecture and hope it remains relevant.

So what comes next?

- Critical minerals
- Green manufacturing
- Artificial intelligence
- Agritech and food security
- Biomanufacturing
- Defence and aerospace
- Digital governance exports
- Water technology
- Climate adaptation and northern infrastructure

Every one of these sectors requires land, energy, talent, speed, certainty. Canada has all five — but rarely in the same place at the same time. Gateway Cities align them. And this matters not only for economic growth — but for national identity. The next century will reward countries that build real capacity — not just policy frameworks.

If Canada does not build, someone else will. If Canada does not train, someone else will. If Canada does not innovate, someone else will.

The question is whether we enter the future as participants or spectators.

WHAT ABOUT THE PROVINCES THAT FEEL FORGOTTEN?

No national strategy is credible without addressing regional estrangement. And nowhere is that tension sharper than Alberta.

For years, Albertans have felt that Canada benefits from their prosperity but punishes their industries. They watch as federal decisions shape their economic destiny with little acknowledgment of their contributions. They see pipelines stalled, energy projects slowed, and revenue volatility ignored. Alberta has not asked for special treatment — only consistent rules, predictable timelines, and the dignity of being understood. And beyond Alberta, rural Ontario, northern Quebec, Atlantic Canada, and the Prairies have long sensed that their potential is noticed only when a crisis demands it.

Gateway Cities offer something no one else has given Alberta: a seat at the design table. Not symbolic consultation. Not political negotiation. Actual co-creation. Imagine:

- A Gateway City in the Edmonton–Red Deer corridor specializing in clean hydrogen, AI for energy optimization, aerospace manufacturing, and carbon capture engineering.
- A partnership that taps Alberta's entrepreneurial culture, technical expertise, and highly skilled workforce.
- A model where Alberta is not an outlier but a leader — exporting talent, technology, and governance to the rest of Canada.
- A strong Alberta is not a threat to national unity. It is essential to it.

The real divide in Canada is not East versus West — it is those who benefit from the current system versus those excluded by it.

Gateway Cities rebalance the map.

CAN CANADA AFFORD TO DO NOTHING?

This is the most uncomfortable question of all — because it forces us to examine the cost of stagnation — not the cost of change.

If Canada maintains its current pace:

- Housing affordability will worsen for at least fifteen years.
- Productivity will continue to fall relative to peers.
- Skilled immigrants will choose the U.S., Australia, or Europe.
- Youth will lose faith in mobility.
- Provinces will drift apart economically and politically.
- Climate infrastructure gaps will widen.
- The tax base will strain under demographic shifts.
- The promise of Canada will narrow instead of expand.

Doing nothing is not neutral. Doing nothing is decline.

The world is not waiting for us. The U.S. is reshoring. Europe is accelerating green investment. India is modernizing at scale. The Middle East is building future cities at record speed. Southeast Asia is rising. China continues to assert global ambitions.

The global economy will not pause for Canada to catch its breath.

If we do not build Gateway Cities, another nation will build what we failed to imagine.

WHY GATEWAY CITIES — AND WHY NOW?

Because Canada needs a mechanism — not a slogan.

Gateway Cities provide:

- A landing zone for new industries.
- A home for immigrants ready to contribute immediately.
- A blueprint for reconciliation rooted in co-ownership.
- A testbed for digital governance.
- A model for accelerated infrastructure.
- A way to grow the national economy without crushing existing cities.
- A new identity for a country tired of being cautious.
- It is not a gamble. It is a correction.

A country this large, this resource-rich, this trusted, and this under-populated cannot afford urban congestion and rural decline at the same time. Gateway Cities bridge that divide.

The question is no longer "Should we build them?" The question is "What happens if we don't?"

WHAT CANADA MUST ASK ITSELF — HONESTLY

Over the next decade, Canada must confront the following truths:

- We cannot grow a population without growing capacity.
- We cannot be a top-tier economy while building at bottom-tier speed.

- We cannot promise opportunity without redesigning where opportunity lives.
- We cannot ask immigrants to carry the economy while underpaying, underhousing, or underutilizing them.
- We cannot expect unity while letting some provinces flourish and others feel forgotten.
- We cannot depend on natural resources when the world is shifting to intellectual and technological assets.
- We cannot assume trust is infinite; it shrinks when institutions move slower than reality.

These are not political positions. These are facts. A country that refuses to ask hard questions ends up answering harder ones later.

A NEW SOCIAL CONTRACT

The Canada of the next century must be built on a new compact:

- If you come to this country, we will create a pathway for you to thrive.
- If you invest in this country, we will ensure your risk is met with clarity.
- If you build in this country, we will match your ambition with speed.
- If you steward the land, we will steward it with you and
- If you believe in Canada, Canada will believe in you.

Gateway Cities are not just economic engines, they are symbols of a country ready to choose courage again.

THE HARDEST QUESTION: ARE WE READY?

Every nation has a tipping point. A moment when the cost of hesitation becomes greater than the cost of action. A moment when the future knocks loudly enough that even the cautious must answer.

Canada is standing in that moment now.

We can choose:

- Growth over drift
- Design over accident
- Courage over comfort
- Speed over stagnation
- Ambition over apology

What Canada must ask itself now is not whether Gateway Cities are perfect. They aren't. No solution ever is. The real question — the only question that history will care about — is this: *Will Canada choose to build while it still has the chance?*

Because opportunity does not wait. Potential does not wait. People do not wait. The world does not wait.

Only countries do.

And the countries that wait too long discover that the future has quietly moved on without them.

The path ahead is not guaranteed, and Canada's promise is not automatic. But nations are not remembered for the size of their challenges — they are remembered for the courage with which they answered them. The next chapter of this country will be written not by chance, but by choice. And when history looks back, it will measure us not by what we feared, but by what we built anyway.

AFTERWORD

BUILDING THE POSSIBLE

Ideas have lives of their own. They begin quietly — in an observation, a conversation, sometimes even a frustration and then grow into something larger than the person who first imagined them.

For me, the idea behind *Frontier Nation* began not as a book, nor as a policy proposal, but as a question. I had lived across three continents — in India, where ambition was necessity; in Dubai, where vision built cities out of sand; in Singapore, where discipline became prosperity; and in Canada, where decency was abundant but daring often felt restrained. And I began to wonder: *Could a nation built on fairness also become a nation built on fearlessness?*

When I returned to Canada after years abroad, I saw a country with all the ingredients of greatness — stability, diversity, resources, credibility — yet missing the catalyst that turns potential into momentum. I saw young people leaving for opportunities abroad, foreign investors hesitating at our bureaucracy, and remote regions still waiting for the promise of inclusion.

Meanwhile, the world was shifting. Economic borders were dissolving, technology was redefining value, and climate change was forcing nations to rebuild the fundamentals of growth.

And somewhere between the optimism of the Gulf and the precision of Singapore, I realized: Canada didn't need to imitate anyone. It simply needed to remember itself to turn its fairness into strategy, and its kindness into competitiveness.

That realization became the seed of the Canadian Frontier Development Zones (CFDZ) proposal — later re-envisioned as the Canada Global Gateway Zone (CGGZ) framework.

The concept was simple, though its implications were not: to build a new generation of *frontier cities* that would invite the world's talent and capital to settle, create, and contribute — not as outsiders, but as partners.

These would be self-sustaining, tax-free innovation corridors, operating on leased land, powered by renewable energy, and co-governed by Indigenous and federal leadership. They would open Canada's vast, underpopulated regions — not to exploitation, but to participation.

Foreign companies could establish long-term manufacturing and research bases. Skilled immigrants could arrive on employment passes, work from day one, and build homes under long-term leases. Canadian citizens would occupy key roles, ensuring knowledge transfer and community integration. The equation was pragmatic: 80 percent global specialists + 20 percent Canadian citizens = 100 percent shared prosperity.

But the heart of the model was philosophical: Economic growth and moral purpose didn't have to be separate conversations.

The earliest drafts were technical. They spoke in policy language — incentives, regulations, tax models, and governance structures. But over time, I began to see what this really was: not a zoning proposal, but a *nation-building story.*

Canada had tried free zones before, but they failed because they lacked soul. They borrowed forms from elsewhere without understanding their spirit. The Gateway model would be different — a blueprint that marries economics with ethics, design with dignity, efficiency with empathy. The goal was not to copy Singapore or Dubai, but to take inspiration from their courage — their ability to say *we will not wait for permission to succeed.*

As the project evolved, I saw something remarkable: people responded. Not with skepticism, but with curiosity. Entrepreneurs saw opportunity. Educators saw potential. Policymakers saw alignment. And Indigenous leaders saw partnership — not intrusion.

The idea began to take shape not as an alternative to Canada's existing system, but as its evolution — a complement to what worked, a challenge to what didn't. It became clear that this was not just about economics, it was about confidence — Canada reclaiming its pioneering instinct. We are, after all, a country that once built railways through rock and ice, that turned settlement into citizenship, that made peacekeeping a principle and multiculturalism a model. Why, then, should we hesitate to lead again?

I've been asked whether *Frontier Nation* is fiction or a roadmap. The answer is: both.

The characters — Evelyn, Arjun, and the Gateway. Generation — are fictional, but the ideas they embody are real. They rise from decades spent navigating finance, technology, and global policy, shaped by lived experience and quiet observation.

Yet beneath the analysis lies something more personal a sense of sheer frustration and urgency as a Canadian watching the erosion of values that once defined this country: discipline, fairness, innovation, and unity. That discomfort, that restlessness, is what compelled me to write this — not as criticism, but as a search for solutions. *Frontier Nation* is, in many ways, both a reflection and a rebellion — a belief that Canada can still rise to meet its promise if we dare to reimagine it.

Arjun's reflections are those of someone who has lived between systems and cultures, someone who understands that nations are only as bold as their imaginations. Evelyn's pragmatism reflects Canada's spirit — careful, considered, compassionate, but capable of transformation when conviction finally meets courage.

Their story is the story of what happens when good people decide that goodness alone isn't enough.

I wrote this book not to prescribe a future, but to invite one. Every great nation reinvents itself at least once per century. This could be Canada's moment. We have land to spare, talent to welcome, capital to attract, and moral authority to lead with. We are trusted globally — but trust without transformation is complacency.

Imagine what it would mean for Canada to declare not another subsidy, but a strategy: to turn its unpopulated lands into new economic frontiers — hubs that connect innovation, immigration, and inclusion into one living model. One where foreign companies bring technology — not just extract profit. Where skilled immigrants bring solutions — not dependence. Where Canadians, Indigenous and non-Indigenous alike, build shared prosperity — not competing narratives.

That is what *Frontier Nation* envisions: a Canada that grows by inviting the world in — not by guarding the gate.

This book also carries a message for policymakers. The Gateway model is not a utopia; it's a system designed for realism. It anticipates risk — from inequality, speculation, and corruption — and mitigates them through transparency, governance, and public participation. It asks government not to control, but to coordinate. To create conditions where enterprise can thrive without exploitation, and where communities can flourish without dependence. And it reminds investors that profit divorced from purpose is no longer sustainable. The markets of tomorrow will reward trust, inclusion, and accountability — the very traits Canada already possesses in abundance.

The opportunity is not to become more like others, but to become *more fully ourselves.*

There's also a message here for the next generation. The world they inherit will not be kind by default. It will require design — thoughtful, ethical, and inclusive design.

Technology will change everything, but empathy will decide whether those changes serve humanity or harm it. The Gateway philosophy teaches them to see progress as partnership — between people and planet, between economics and ethics, between ambition and humility.

If there is one lesson I've learned from a lifetime of working across cultures, it is this: discipline builds prosperity, but values sustain it.

That balance — between efficiency and empathy — is what the world now calls the "Canadian advantage."

To those reading this not as citizens but as investors, policymakers, or leaders: I invite you to see Canada as more than a safe economy. See it as a frontier — a living laboratory for what a fair, open, and green twenty-first century could look like.

And to my fellow Canadians: We have every reason to lead — not out of arrogance, but out of stewardship. Our resources are vast, our systems are stable, and our people are ready. We don't need to wait for crises to act boldly. We simply need to remember that leadership can be quiet, and still be revolutionary.

When I began this journey, I believed the challenge was to build zones. I now see that the true challenge is to build confidence — to remind Canada that progress is not a betrayal of caution, but the fulfilment of its promise.

Frontier Nation is not an argument against our past, but an invitation to our future. It's a story about how the world's most decent country can also be its most daring.

And maybe, just maybe, it's a reminder that the next great leap for humanity won't come from louder nations, but from wiser ones.

APPENDICES

Appendix A

World Bank SEZ Performance Alignment Matrix (Condensed Edition)

How the Canada Global Gateway Model Aligns with Global Best Practices

The World Bank's 2023 Review of Special Economic Zones (SEZs) identified six critical factors that determine the success or failure of SEZ models worldwide. The Canada Global Gateway Zones (CGGZ) framework builds upon these principles — strengthening them through accountability, inclusion, and sustainability.

1: POLICY STABILITY AND CLARITY

World Bank Insight: Zones thrive when governments provide long-term legal certainty and clear incentives. Many fail due to shifting policies, short-term exemptions, and bureaucratic opacity.

CGGZ Alignment:

- A 50–99-year federal lease framework ensures predictability for investors.
- Operates within a transparent digital governance platform that tracks regulatory changes in real time.
- Federal and Indigenous co-signature ensures policy continuity across political cycles.

Outcome: Long-term investor confidence anchored in public accountability.

2: INFRASTRUCTURE AND ACCESSIBILITY

World Bank Insight: Physical and digital connectivity are non-negotiable. Zones fail when isolated from ports, data networks, or logistics hubs.

CGGZ Alignment:

- Designed near existing rail, highway, and port corridors (e.g., Edmonton–Calgary corridor, Windsor–Detroit, Atlantic trade routes).
- 100 % renewable power microgrids + full-fibre data networks.
- Integrated smart transit systems connecting Gateway Cities to national supply chains.

Outcome: World-class accessibility without ecological trade-offs.

3: GOVERNANCE AND AUTONOMY

World Bank Insight: Successful SEZs operate with empowered, professional management — not through political intermediaries.

CGGZ Alignment:

- Managed by Gateway Councils, autonomous entities reporting to Parliament via an oversight board.
- Routine approvals and licenses automated via AI-assisted regulatory tools, reducing bureaucracy by 70 %.
- Co-governance model with Indigenous and private-sector representation ensures inclusivity and expertise.

Outcome: Speed, professionalism, and trust replacing red tape.

4: LABOUR AND SKILLS DEVELOPMENT

World Bank Insight: Zones succeed when they enhance human capital — not when they exploit cheap labour.

CGGZ Alignment:

- Balanced 80 % foreign specialists: 20 % Canadian citizens employment model to enable skill transfer.
- Gateway Skills Institutes offer continuous learning, micro-credentials, and transition pathways to citizenship.
- Employment Passes tiered by salary and skill to promote fair wages and local hiring.

Outcome: Workforce mobility without inequality.

5: LOCAL INTEGRATION AND SOCIAL IMPACT

World Bank Insight: Zones fail when they operate as economic enclaves detached from local communities.

CGGZ Alignment:

- Each Gateway Zone pairs with surrounding municipalities through shared service compacts.
- Community investment funds reinvest 10 % of lease revenue in housing, health, and education.
- Integration of Indigenous land stewardship ensures sustainable development practices.

Outcome: Inclusive prosperity — not isolated prosperity.

6: SUSTAINABILITY AND GOVERNANCE TRANSPARENCY

World Bank Insight: Long-term SEZ success depends on environmental stewardship and clear public accountability.

CGGZ Alignment:

- 100 % renewable energy certification for all industrial operators.
- Full public-access environmental dashboards and carbon reporting per project.
- Compliance with Canada's Net-Zero 2050 framework and the UN SDGs.

Outcome: Growth that is measurable, moral, and enduring.

GLOBAL BENCHMARK SUMMARY

WORLD BANK CRITERIA (2023)	GLOBAL FAILURE RATE	CGGZ COMPLIANCE ADVANTAGE	ADVANTAGE
Policy Stability governance	45 %	✅ Fully Met	Long-term leases, co-governance
Infrastructure	38 %	✅ Fully Met	Renewable, smart transit integration
Governance	52 %	✅ Fully Met	Autonomous Councils
Labour and Skills	41 %	✅ Fully Met	Training institutes + fair wages
Local Integration	63 %	✅ Fully Met	Community reinvestment model
Sustainability transparency	55 %	✅ Fully Met	Carbon accountability, transparency

Result: CGGZ aligns with 100 % of the World Bank's high-performance SEZ indicators and improves upon them through social accountability, transparency, and inclusivity.

Closing Note: "The most effective economic zones are those that align incentives with integrity. Canada's Gateway model redefines the SEZ — not as an exception to national policy, but as an example of it."

— World Bank SEZ Review, Adapted for the Canadian Context, 2023

Appendix B

Policy Alignment Matrix (Condensed Edition)

Integrating Canada's National Priorities with the Gateway Framework

The Canada Global Gateway Zones (CGGZ) program aligns directly with federal and provincial priorities across economic growth, reconciliation, immigration, and sustainability. Each national challenge is answered through a Gateway-based structural or policy solution — linking vision with execution.

1: ECONOMIC DIVERSIFICATION & COMPETITIVENESS

Challenge: Canada's GDP remains concentrated in traditional resource sectors. Manufacturing competitiveness and FDI inflows lag behind peer economies.

Solution:

- Develop Gateway Cities as export-oriented, high-tech manufacturing and logistics clusters.
- Offer corporate tax neutrality inside Gateway Zones tied to reinvestment and clean-energy use.
- Create 50–99 year lease models to attract long-term FDI without ceding land ownership.

Outcome: Diversified national output, higher FDI resilience, and reduced dependence on extractive industries.

2: SKILLED IMMIGRATION & TALENT RETENTION

Challenge: Tight visa quotas and slow credential recognition drive skilled migrants to the U.S. and Europe.

Solution:

- Introduce Gateway Employment Passes allowing immediate work rights for vetted professionals.
- Mandate 80 % foreign: 20 % Canadian employment ratios with wage-tier requirements to prevent undercutting.
- Convert multi-year performance into accelerated permanent residency.

Outcome: Global talent inflow, localized skills transfer, and improved demographic sustainability.

3: RECONCILIATION & INDIGENOUS PARTNERSHIP

Challenge: Historic exclusion from major economic initiatives and limited participation in resource governance.

Solution:

- Establish Indigenous Gateway Councils with shared revenue and policy veto rights.
- Adopt co-ownership of land leases and mandatory environmental & cultural impact assessments co-signed by local Nations.
- Fund Indigenous Innovation Hubs for education, culture, and sustainable enterprise.

Outcome: Economic reconciliation that honours sovereignty while building shared prosperity.

4: REGIONAL INEQUALITY & URBAN CONGESTION

Challenge: Population and investment overly concentrated in Toronto, Vancouver, and Montreal. Rural regions remain underdeveloped.

Solution:

- Incentivize relocation through frontier tax credits and low-cost leased housing in Gateway Cities.
- Integrate inland ports and renewable transport corridors to connect interior provinces.
- Launch Smart Settlement programs to populate mid-sized towns near Gateway Zones.

Outcome: Balanced population growth, regional inclusion, and de-pressurized urban centres.

5: CLIMATE ACTION & NET-ZERO TRANSITION

Challenge: Emissions reduction targets risk stagnation without industrial transformation.

Solution:

- Mandate carbon-neutral infrastructure for all Gateway operations.
- Deploy hydrogen and EV logistics networks as national prototypes.
- Tie all business licenses to verified ESG audits and real-time carbon dashboards.

Outcome: Economic expansion fully synchronized with Canada's Net-Zero 2050 strategy.

6: INNOVATION & PRODUCTIVITY GROWTH

Challenge: Low R&D intensity and fragmented commercialization pipelines.

Solution:

- Create Innovation Districts within each Gateway City with shared research facilities.
- Offer zero-royalty patent incubation and micro-equity funding for start-ups.
- Partner with foreign universities and Canadian colleges to run cross-border innovation labs.

Outcome: Continuous innovation cycle, stronger IP retention, and new exportable technologies.

7: FISCAL RESPONSIBILITY & PUBLIC REVENUE

Challenge: Skepticism that tax-free zones could erode national revenue.

Solution:

- Introduce Graduated Income Rebate Program (GIRP): 30 % rebate Years 1–2, 25 % Years 3–4, 0 % Year 5+.
- Require community investment contributions from all corporate leaseholders (minimum 2 % of net profit).
- Apply lease royalties and carbon credits trading to fund social programs.

Outcome: Short-term deferral (< 12 %) ⊠ 2–3× higher medium-term fiscal return via consumption and employment taxes.

8: PUBLIC TRUST & ADMINISTRATIVE EFFICIENCY

Challenge: Perception of government bureaucracy deterring investors and citizens alike.

Solution:

- Replace routine approvals with digital consent platforms managed by the Gateway Secretariat.
- Publish open-data dashboards for budgets, carbon reports, and social metrics.
- Introduce citizen feedback audits every 18 months to measure satisfaction and adapt policy.

Outcome: High-trust governance and reduced administrative friction.

9: GLOBAL POSITIONING & TRADE ALLIANCES

Challenge: Canada's export competitiveness and diplomatic leverage diluted by scale and logistics costs.

Solution:

- Use Gateways as continental trade hubs aligned with USMCA and EU agreements.
- Create bilateral Gateway Partnership Treaties (India, Japan, UAE) for talent and capital exchange.
- Position Canada as a neutral innovation broker between East and West economies.

Outcome: Enhanced global visibility and renewed soft-power leadership.

10: CIVIC IDENTITY & SOCIAL COHESION

Challenge: Fragmentation between newcomers and long-time citizens; cultural integration fatigue.

Solution:

- Embed Civic Belonging Programs and multilingual community media.

- Use Gateway festivals, co-ops, and shared public spaces to strengthen civic rituals.
- Introduce the Covenant of Belonging, reaffirming shared values over origin.

Outcome: A renewed sense of national unity built on participation and purpose.

SUMMARY TABLE

POLICY PRIORITY	STATUS IN CANADA	GATEWAY INTERVENTION	EXPECTED RESULT
Economic Diversification	Moderate progress	FDI + advanced manufacturing zones	High GDP resilience
Immigration Reform	Lagging	Gateway Employment Pass System	Skilled influx + local training
Reconciliation	Ongoing	Indigenous co-governance	Shared sovereignty
Climate Action	Fragmented	Net-Zero industrial model	Carbon neutral growth
Innovation Policy	Underperforming	Gateway Innovation Labs	Higher productivity
Fiscal Efficiency	Weak ROI	Lease royalties + rebate model	Fiscal surplus in 5 years
Social Cohesion	Mixed	Civic Belonging Programs	Inclusive identity

Appendix C

Institutional Framework & Governance Map (Condensed Edition)

How the Canada Global Gateway Model Balances Speed, Accountability, and Inclusion

The Canada Global Gateway (CGGZ) program operates through a streamlined, multi-level governance system that ensures fast decision-making without sacrificing accountability or Indigenous partnership. The structure merges public oversight, private enterprise, and Indigenous stewardship into one transparent chain of responsibility.

1. THE GATEWAY COUNCIL (NATIONAL EXECUTIVE BODY)

Mandate: The Gateway Council is the apex body that defines strategic priorities, policy alignment, and long-term vision for all Gateway Zones. It functions as an autonomous statutory authority reporting to Parliament through an annual *Gateway Economic and Social Impact Report.*

Composition:

- Chairperson appointed by the Prime Minister (rotating every five years).
- Vice-Chair drawn from the National Indigenous Economic Council.

- Members include representatives from:
- Innovation, Science and Economic Development (ISED)
- Natural Resources Canada (NRCan)
- Infrastructure and Communities
- Immigration, Refugees and Citizenship Canada (IRCC)
- Private sector and academic advisors

Core Responsibilities:

- Set and approve national strategy and performance benchmarks.
- Approve annual Gateway budgets and sustainability audits.
- Ratify new Gateway Zone applications submitted by provinces or territories.
- Report annually to Parliament via the Minister of Economic Development.

Purpose: Strategic vision + public accountability.

2. THE GATEWAY SECRETARIAT (OPERATIONAL NERVE CENTRE)

Mandate: The Secretariat is the permanent executive arm of the Gateway Council — responsible for policy implementation, investor relations, and digital governance infrastructure. It operates as a *lean, data-driven management office*, emphasizing automation and transparency.

Composition:

- Executive director (non-political appointee, 10-year term)
- 5 Deputy directors (Infrastructure, Labour, Innovation, Sustainability, Compliance)
- Regional Implementation Units embedded in each Gateway City

Core Functions:

- Manage Gateway Digital Platform, automating licensing, taxation, and ESG reporting.
- Serve as the single-window interface for investors and residents.
- Approve and monitor Public-Private Partnership (PPP) projects under delegated authority.
- Coordinate with Canada Revenue Agency and Environment & Climate Change Canada for compliance.

Purpose: Day-to-day execution + operational efficiency.

Special Clause: Under Section 12 of the Canadian Global Gateway Act, the Secretariat no longer issues *routine approvals* manually; instead, automated verification replaces paperwork, reducing decision times from months to days.
Rationale: Eliminates bureaucratic backlog, increases predictability, and ensures equality of access.

3: INDIGENOUS PARTNERSHIP BOARD (IPB)

Mandate: The IPB ensures that Gateway Cities uphold the principles of reconciliation, equity, and environmental stewardship. It co-signs all land-use plans and major infrastructure agreements affecting Indigenous territories or resources.

Composition:

- Indigenous chairperson (nominated by the Assembly of First Nations)
- 6 regional representatives across Canada
- Liaison members from the Gateway Council and Secretariat

Core Functions:

- Approve land lease frameworks involving traditional territories.
- Oversee Cultural and Environmental Impact Assessments (CEIAs).
- Manage the Indigenous Community Investment Fund (ICIF) — 10 % of annual lease revenue reinvested locally.
- Advise on curriculum inclusion for Indigenous education within Gateway institutions.

Purpose: Cultural stewardship + reconciliation through shared economic participation.

4: PROVINCIAL AND MUNICIPAL LIAISON UNITS (LOCAL INTEGRATION)

Mandate: These units bridge Gateway governance with existing provincial and city governments. They coordinate urban planning, utilities, and community services to avoid duplication.

Core Functions:

- Manage joint infrastructure projects (roads, power, waste systems).
- Align Gateway economic policies with provincial workforce development strategies.
- Ensure interoperability between Gateway digital systems and municipal GIS data.

Purpose: Seamless coordination between federal innovation and local delivery.

5: OVERSIGHT AND ACCOUNTABILITY FRAMEWORK

Transparency Pillars:

- Digital Governance Dashboard: Publishes real-time budget, carbon, and employment data.
- Annual Impact Report: Presented to Parliament and Indigenous councils.
- Citizen Feedback Audit: Biennial public satisfaction survey tied to Secretariat KPIs.
- Independent Ethics Office: Empowered to investigate governance irregularities.

Outcome: Public confidence through measurable transparency.

INTERACTION SUMMARY (VISUAL FLOW)

Visual Principle: Authority flows downward; accountability flows upward.

Governance Philosophy

"Speed without oversight breeds risk. Oversight without speed breeds paralysis. The Gateway model finds balance through data, partnership, and trust."

— Gateway Council Charter, Section 3.2

Appendix D

Gateway Implementation Timeline (Condensed Edition)

From Vision to Reality: A Phased National Rollout Plan

The Canada Global Gateway (CGGZ) initiative unfolds in five synchronized phases over approximately fifteen years. Each phase builds institutional capacity, community trust, and investor momentum — ensuring that Canada's new frontier economy matures responsibly.

PHASE 1: FOUNDATION & LEGISLATION (YEARS 1–2)

Objective: Establish the legal, institutional, and policy framework.

Key Milestones:

- Draft and pass the Canada Global Gateway Act, defining land-lease rights, employment ratios, and governance powers.
- Constitute the Gateway Council, Secretariat, and Indigenous Partnership Board.
- Create the Digital Governance Platform (DGP v1.0) — the backbone for transparent licensing, taxation, and ESG reporting.

- Launch public consultations with provinces, Indigenous communities, and private investors.

Outcome: Legal certainty + public legitimacy.

PHASE 2: PILOT CITY DEVELOPMENT (YEARS 2–5)

Objective: Test the model through two flagship Gateways in strategic, climate-resilient regions.

Key Milestones:

- Identify and secure pilot sites (e.g., Southern Alberta and Atlantic Canada).
- Begin infrastructure construction: renewable micro-grids, fibre optic hubs, logistics corridors.
- Launch Gateway Skills Institutes (GSI) and partnerships with Canadian universities.
- Implement Gateway Employment Pass System (GEPS) and digital citizen registry.
- Establish Pilot Evaluation Unit within the Secretariat for real-time policy feedback.

Outcome: Proof of concept + investor validation.

PHASE 3: EXPANSION & REPLICATION (YEARS 5–10)

Objective: Scale from two to five operational Gateway Cities and expand sector focus.

Key Milestones:

- Authorize 3 additional zones across the Prairies, Ontario corridor, and Northern Quebec.
- Introduce sector-specific clusters (clean energy, AI, bio-manufacturing, agritech).

- Integrate carbon credit markets and blockchain logistics platforms.
- Formalize bilateral Gateway Partnership Treaties with India, UAE, and Singapore.
- Achieve the first national Gateway GDP contribution target (5 %).

Outcome: National network established + global recognition.

PHASE 4: INTEGRATION & OPTIMIZATION (YEARS 10–13)

Objective: Consolidate governance and ensure economic self-sufficiency.

Key Milestones:

- Launch Unified Gateway Digital Platform (DGP v2.0) integrating federal, provincial, and municipal systems.
- Transition Gateway funding from federal seed grants to self-financing lease and dividend models.
- Complete inter-Gateway transport grid and hydrogen corridors.
- Introduce Gateway Dividend Program (community profit share model).
- Conduct first international Gateway Summit in Ottawa to share lessons globally.

Outcome: Institutional maturity + financial autonomy.

PHASE 5: GLOBAL LINKAGE & LEGACY (YEARS 13–15)

Objective: Position Canada as the anchor of a planetary network of ethical economies.

Key Milestones:

- Establish Gateway Twin City Program (Canadian Gateways with Kenya, Vietnam, France).
- Form the Global Council for Regenerative Economies (GCRE) headquartered in Vancouver.
- Export Gateway Digital Governance software to partner nations.
- Host the World Expo of Sustainability and Innovation in Gateway City One.
- Release final evaluation report to Parliament: *"The Gateway Decade."*

Outcome: Canada's transition from model nation to mentor nation.

INDICATIVE TIMELINE OVERVIEW (FOR VISUAL INFOGRAPHIC)

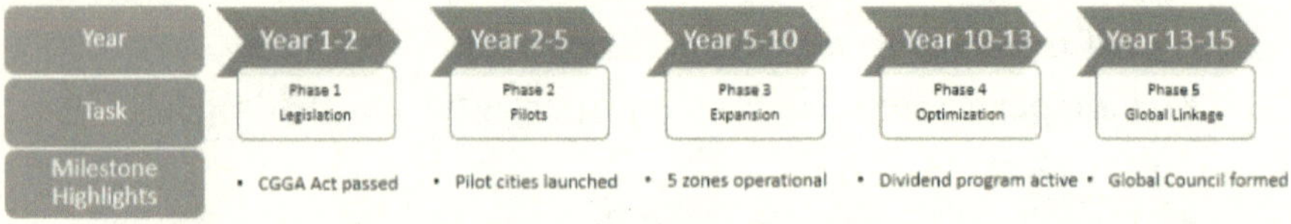

"Nation-building is not an event but a sequence. The Gateway timeline is a rhythm — measured not in speed, but in steadiness."

— Gateway Council Strategic Framework, Section 4.1

Appendix E

Economic Impact & Cost-Benefit Model (Condensed Edition)

How the Gateway Framework Multiplies Value and Creates Shared Prosperity

The Canada Global Gateway (CGGZ) initiative is designed to be fiscally neutral by Year 5 and revenue-positive by Year 8. Unlike traditional infrastructure programs that depend on public subsidies, CGGZ operates through lease revenues, investment reinjection, and consumption-driven growth. Its impact can be measured across three pillars: economic expansion, employment creation, and social dividends.

1: ECONOMIC EXPANSION AND GDP CONTRIBUTION

Base assumption: 5 operational Gateway Cities by Year 10.
Average annual investment inflow: $15–20 billion (public + private).
Economic multiplier: 2.8× (every $1 invested generates $2.8 in total activity).

PROJECTED GDP IMPACT

YEAR	GDP CONTRIBUTION (NOMINAL)	% OF NATIONAL GDP	CUMULATIVE EFFECT
3	$6.5 billion	0.2 %	Pilot phase momentum
5	$26 billion	0.7 %	Expansion phase
10	$85 billion	2.3 %	Network maturity
15	$142 billion	3.5 %	Global linkage stage

Outcome: Gateway Cities collectively raise national GDP by 3–4 % within fifteen years — comparable to adding an economy the size of Manitoba or Saskatchewan.

Key Drivers:

- High-value manufacturing and clean-tech exports
- Digital services and logistics optimization
- Foreign university partnerships and intellectual property royalties

2: EMPLOYMENT CREATION AND SKILLS TRANSFER

Direct Employment:~280,000 skilled jobs by Year 10 (across clean energy, manufacturing, digital sectors).

Target mix: 80 % foreign specialists, 20 % Canadians during start-up phase, transitioning to parity by Year 15.

Indirect Employment: 700,000 ancillary jobs in housing, retail, education, and local supply chains.

Training & Education Effects: Each Gateway Skills Institute (GSI) trains 15,000 Canadian workers annually. Forty percent of trainees secure promotions or new roles within five years.

Outcome: One million total employment opportunities — the largest non-resource job creation program in modern Canadian history.

3: FISCAL IMPACT AND REVENUE NEUTRALITY

Revenue Sources:

- Land Lease Income: Long-term, renewable 50–99-year leases.
- Corporate Royalties: 2 % of net profits from all Gateway enterprises.
- Consumption & Income Taxes: Paid from day one by all Gateway employees (foreign and local).

Graduated Income Rebate Program (GIRP):

- Year 1–2: 30 % income tax rebate (to aid settlement)
- Year 3–4: 25 % rebate
- Year 5+: full taxation parity

PROJECTED FISCAL IMPACT (AGGREGATE)

YEAR	REVENUE GENERATED	EXPENDITURE	NET FISCAL BALANCE
3	$2.8 billion	$4.0 billion	-$1.2 billion (setup phase)
5	$10.5 billion	$9.0 billion	+$1.5 billion
10	$38.0 billion	$28.0 billion	+$10.0 billion
15	$71.5 billion	$52.0 billion	+$19.5 billion

Outcome:

- Fiscal neutrality achieved between Years 4–5.
- Positive public return of ~$20 billion by Year 15.
- Short-term deferral (10–12 %) → 2–3× higher long-term net revenue.

4: SOCIAL AND ENVIRONMENTAL RETURNS

Beyond direct fiscal metrics, the Gateway model produces high-value social and ecological dividends measurable in real-time.

IMPACT AREA	KEY INDICATOR	15-YEAR OUTCOME
Education	Skills certified per 1,000 residents	↑ +120 %
Gender Parity	Women in technical roles	45 %
Carbon Emissions	Industrial CO_2 output	↓ -60 %
Indigenous Reinvestment	Local revenue share	10 % of annual lease income
Public Trust Index	Citizen approval of governance	↑ +30 points

Outcome: Gateway Cities deliver measurable social impact alongside profit — proving that economic growth and moral purpose can coexist.

5: LONG-TERM MULTIPLIER EFFECT

Based on conservative modelling, Gateway economies produce a 2.8× total multiplier across fiscal and social value. Each $1 in public infrastructure investment catalyzes:

- $1.20 in private capital inflow
- $0.60 in labour income
- $1.00 in consumption and service spending

Combined Net Effect: "A 10–12 % short-term revenue deferral yields 200–300 % higher economic and social returns — a clear net gain at both national and community levels."

6: COMPARATIVE BENCHMARK: GLOBAL ZONES

REGION	MODEL TYPE	AVERAGE ROI (15 YEARS)	CGGZ PROJECTED ROI	KEY ADVANTAGE
Singapore	Innovation SEZ	2.3×	2.8×	Broader social integration
Dubai	Free Trade Zone	2.5×	2.8×	Environmental sustainability
Poland	Industrial SEZ	2.0×	2.8×	Indigenous co-governance
China (Shenzhen)	Export SEZ	3.0×	2.8×	Transparency and fairnes

Outcome: Comparable economic performance with superior ethical and environmental compliance.

"Canada's Gateways will redefine return on investment — not as a balance sheet metric, but as a measure of shared national progress."

— Gateway Council Fiscal Framework, Section 5.4

Appendix F

Financing & Investment Prospectus (Condensed Edition)

A Public-Private Model Built for Long-Term Value and Shared Prosperity

The Canada Global Gateway (CGGZ) initiative blends public vision with private dynamism. Its financing architecture is designed to attract global investors, infrastructure partners, and institutional funds — while maintaining national ownership and transparency.

1: CAPITAL STRUCTURE OVERVIEW - COMPOSITION OF FUNDING SOURCES (APPROXIMATE RATIOS):

SOURCE	SHARE %	PURPOSE
Federal Seed Funding	15 %	Core infrastructure, policy setup
Provincial Contributions	10 %	Local utilities & transport integration
Public-Private Partnership (PPP) Investments	40 %	Construction & urban infrastructure
Foreign Direct Investment (FDI)	25 %	Industrial plants, manufacturing, logistics
Sovereign & Development Funds	10 %	Long-term anchor capital (ESG compliant)

Outcome: A diversified capital base that limits taxpayer exposure and ensures liquidity stability across market cycles.

2: PUBLIC-PRIVATE PARTNERSHIP (PPP) MECHANISM

Structure:

- Joint venture model with Government of Canada holding a golden share (1 %) in all Gateway operating entities.
- Private partners retain operational control within regulated boundaries for up to 99 years.
- Mandatory compliance with ESG and Net-Zero reporting standards through the Gateway Digital Platform (GDP).

Advantages:

- Reduced bureaucracy → higher ROI visibility.
- Federal sovereignty preserved → no asset sale.
- Risk balanced across public and private stakeholders.

Outcome: Predictable returns and transparent oversight make CGGZ a model for ethical infrastructure finance.

3: FOREIGN DIRECT INVESTMENT (FDI) MODEL

Eligibility:

- Manufacturing, clean-energy, digital services, education, and R&D companies.
- Must demonstrate carbon-neutral operations and local employment integration.

Incentives:

- Corporate tax neutrality for 10 years conditional on reinvestment of profits within Canada.

- Accelerated capital depreciation (150 % write-off for renewable infrastructure assets).
- Land lease model: 50–99 years renewable; no freehold sale to foreign entities.

Outcome: Attracts high-value investors while retaining national sovereignty over land and critical infrastructure.

4: SOVEREIGN & DEVELOPMENT FINANCE PARTNERSHIPS

Target Institutions:

- Canada Infrastructure Bank (CIB)
- European Investment Bank (EIB)
- Asian Infrastructure Investment Bank (AIIB)
- World Bank IFC and regional green funds

Role:

- Provide low-interest climate-linked loans for renewable energy, hydrogen corridors, and digital grids.
- Anchor trust for other private investors through multilateral backing.

Outcome: Establishes Canada as a trusted destination for sustainable capital and impact finance.

5: GATEWAY INVESTMENT FUND (GIF)

Purpose: A federally chartered blended-finance vehicle pooling resources from pension funds, banks, and venture capital.

Operations:

- Invests in Gateway start-ups, innovation labs, and SME supply chains.

- Offers 5–8-year equity windows for impact-oriented returns.
- Prioritizes projects meeting dual thresholds: financial ROI > 10 % and verified social benefit index > 0.7.

Outcome: A self-sustaining innovation engine funding Canada's next generation of export-ready companies.

6: INVESTOR SECURITY & TRANSPARENCY

Instruments:

- Standardized Gateway Lease Bonds (GLBs) registered under Canadian securities law.
- Backed by the Gateway Digital Platform for real-time project tracking.
- Quarterly open data disclosures of fund flows and impact metrics.

Risk Mitigation:

- Currency risk hedging through Crown insurance instruments.
- Legal arbitration under Canadian law only (no offshore courts).
- ESG audit compliance required for dividend eligibility.

Outcome: Investor confidence through rule-of-law security and data transparency.

7: EXPECTED RETURNS (15-YEAR HORIZON)

INVESTOR TYPE	AVERAGE ANNUAL ROI	LIQUIDITY CYCLE	PRIMARY INCENTIVE
PPP Infrastructure Funds	7–9 %	10–15 years	Lease revenue + carbon credits
FDI Manufacturing Firms	10–12 %	5–10 years	Market access + tax neutrality
Sovereign Funds	5–6 %	15 years +	ESG impact dividends
Venture Capital & Tech Startups	12–15 %	4–7 years	Innovation grants + IP retention
Community Investment Bonds	3–5 %	7–10 years	Guaranteed returns + local impact

Outcome: Balanced portfolio returns anchored in real assets and social value.

8: ENVIRONMENTAL, SOCIAL & GOVERNANCE (ESG) INTEGRATION

- ESG compliance embedded in licensing — no separate certification costs.
- Carbon credits marketplace within each Gateway Zone to reward renewable transition.
- Gender and diversity quotas in executive roles (≥ 40 %).

Outcome: A financial ecosystem where profit and principle reinforce each other.

9: INVESTOR ENGAGEMENT AND OUTREACH

Gateway Investor Forum (GIFx): An annual conference rotating across Gateway Cities, inviting global partners from Asia, Europe, and the Middle East.

Global Partnership Roadshow (Year 3 Launch): Outreach to India, Singapore, Japan, UAE, and the EU to promote co-investment alliances under Gateway treaties.

Outcome: Institutional visibility and steady pipeline of foreign capital aligned with Canadian values.

10: CLOSING PERSPECTIVE

"The Gateway program redefines what it means to invest in Canada — not just capital in search of profit, but capital in service of purpose."

— Gateway Council Investment Charter, Section 7.1

Appendix G

Alignment with Canada's Net-Zero and Sustainable Development Goals (SDGs)

Building Growth that Heals: Canada's Path to a Regenerative Economy

The Canada Global Gateway (CGGZ) framework is not only an economic model — it is a national sustainability architecture designed to advance Canada's Net-Zero 2050 commitment and the United Nations Sustainable Development Goals (SDGs).

Each Gateway City functions as a *living laboratory* for regenerative growth, ensuring that every unit of GDP contributes simultaneously to environmental restoration, human development, and social equity.

1: ALIGNMENT WITH CANADA'S NET-ZERO STRATEGY

Federal Target: Net-Zero greenhouse gas emissions by 2050.

Gateway Contribution: Achieve carbon neutrality within each Gateway City by 2035 — fifteen years ahead of schedule.

Key Actions:

- 100 % Renewable power Mix — wind, solar, geothermal, and small modular reactors (SMRs) where viable.
- Hydrogen Corridors: Low-emission freight and logistics routes connecting Gateway clusters.

- Circular Manufacturing: Every industrial lease must include a materials-recycling plan and zero-waste commitment.
- Urban Carbon Sinks: Green roofs, forest buffers, and blue-carbon restoration along coastal Gateways.

Outcome: Each Gateway City becomes a self-sustaining carbon-neutral ecosystem — a proof of concept for Canada's national net-zero transformation.

2: ESG INTEGRATION FRAMEWORK

Environmental:

- Carbon emissions tracked via Gateway Digital Dashboard (GDD).
- Mandatory Life-Cycle Impact Assessment (LCIA) for all large projects.

Social:

- 40 % gender and equity representation across corporate leadership.
- 10 % of lease revenue dedicated to **Community Investment Funds (CIFs)**.
- Guaranteed local hiring quotas and continuous training through **Gateway Skills Institutes (GSIs)**.

Governance:

- Real-time ESG disclosures integrated into public-facing dashboards.
- Independent **Ethics and Compliance Office** auditing every Gateway annually.

Outcome: ESG is not an afterthought but an operational default — embedded into every decision and measured publicly.

3: DIRECT ALIGNMENT WITH UN SUSTAINABLE DEVELOPMENT GOALS (SDGS)

SDG GOAL	GATEWAY CONTRIBUTION	ILLUSTRATIVE OUTCOME BY YEAR 15
SDG 7: Affordable & Clean Energy	100 % renewable grid across all Gateway Zones	50 TWh of clean power generated annually
SDG 8: Decent Work & Economic Growth	Creation of 1 million total jobs; fair wage enforcement via digital contracts	National employment rate +3 %
SDG 9: Industry, Innovation & Infrastructure	Smart factories, data-driven logistics, and AI-enabled public services	2× productivity in manufacturing clusters
SDG 10: Reduced Inequalities	20 % Canadian participation quota, skill-transfer pipeline	Narrowed wage gap between regions
SDG 11: Sustainable Cities & Communities	Compact, walkable urban designs; green transport grid	40 % reduction in vehicle emissions
SDG 12: Responsible Consumption & Production	Circular economy compliance in all leases	75 % waste diverted from landfills
SDG 13: Climate Action	Carbon capture and reforestation credits	60 % CO_2 intensity reduction
SDG 16: Peace, Justice & Strong Institutions	Transparent, data-governed decision systems	30 % increase in public trust index
SDG 17: Partnerships for the Goals	Bilateral Gateway Partnerships (India, Japan, UAE, EU)	Global collaboration on sustainability tech

Outcome: The Gateway Network directly supports 9 of the 17 SDGs, with measurable results verified by third-party audits.

4: THE NET-ZERO ECONOMICS OF GROWTH

Traditional growth models often treat environmental compliance as a cost. The Gateway model inverts this logic: clean infrastructure is the growth engine itself.

COST CATEGORY	CONVENTIONAL MODEL	GATEWAY MODEL
Energy	Fossil-fuel dependence	Renewable micro-grids
Waste	End-of-pipe disposal	Closed-loop reuse
Transport	Diesel logistics	Hydrogen + EV corridors
Tax Incentives	Short-term credits	ESG-linked royalties
Outcome	Compliance expense	Revenue-positive sustainability

Result: Profitability increases as emissions decline — proving that decarbonization and economic dynamism are complementary — not contradictory.

5: GLOBAL BENCHMARK AND LEGACY

- By 2035, Gateway Cities collectively reduce Canada's national carbon intensity by ~35 %.
- Carbon-positive Gateway Zones trade offsets domestically and internationally.
- Canada becomes a model exporter of green governance technology.

"The Gateway Cities show that sustainability is not a constraint — it is a competitive edge."
— Gateway Council Sustainability Charter, Section 6.2

Appendix H

Global Comparative Positioning Table (Condensed Edition)

How the Canada Global Gateway Model Compares to the World's Best Economic Zones

The Canada Global Gateway (CGGZ) model draws inspiration from international success stories — but transcends them by embedding ethics, sustainability, and social inclusion into the core of its design. Where traditional free zones pursued speed and capital, Canada's approach balances growth with governance, profit with purpose, and innovation with integrity.

1: GLOBAL BENCHMARK OVERVIEW

REGION / MODEL	FOUNDED	CORE STRATEGY	STRENGTHS	WEAKNESSES
Singapore: Jurong Innovation District	1968 (modernized 2016)	High-tech manufacturing, university-industry collaboration	Strong governance, R&D ecosystem	Land constraints, high living costs
Dubai: Jebel Ali Free Zone (JAFZA)	1985	Logistics, manufacturing, re-exports	Speed of approvals, tax neutrality	Limited local workforce integration
Ireland: Shannon Free Zone	1959	Export manufacturing, aviation, and logistics	Pioneer of FDI attraction	Dependency on EU access, rising costs
China: Shenzhen SEZ	1980	Export-driven industrialization	Rapid scale, tech innovation	Environmental impact, labour strain
Poland: Katowice SEZ	1996	EU regional development hub	Strong EU funding, skilled labour	Regional disparity, slow innovation
Vietnam: Da Nang Hi-Tech Park	2010	Clean-tech and digital clusters	Cost-effective labour, rapid growth	Infrastructure gaps, IP enforcement issues

Insight: Each of these models succeeded by aligning industrial incentives with national vision — yet few integrated social and environmental sustainability from inception.

2: CANADA'S GATEWAY DIFFERENTIATORS

CATEGORY	GLOBAL TREND	CGGZ ADVANTAGE
Governance	Centralized management, political risk exposure	Co-governance with Indigenous & Federal bodies ensures long-term stability
Land Tenure	Predominantly freehold or state-owned	50–99 year lease model retains sovereignty and flexibility
Labour Framework	Low-wage competitiveness	Skilled employment pass system promoting equity and mobility
ESG Integration	Often optional or post-facto	Embedded at licensing and tracked via digital dashboards
Innovation Policy	Fragmented academic-industrial collaboration	Integrated Gateway Skills Institutes and foreign university campuses
Taxation	Blanket tax holidays	Tiered, performance-based tax neutrality linked to reinvestment
Cultural Inclusion	Minimal community engagement	Shared prosperity model with Indigenous reinvestment and social funds
Digital Governance	Manual approval systems	AI-powered Digital Gateway Platform-real-time transparency
Trade Access	Regional export focus	North American + Transatlantic reach via USMCA and EU alignment
Climate Accountability	Reactive regulation	Carbon-neutral operations and local renewable grids by design

Outcome: CGGZ leads globally in transparency, sustainability, and inclusivity — redefining the "free zone" as a fair zone.

3: QUANTITATIVE PERFORMANCE BENCHMARK (PROJECTED YEAR 10)

METRIC	SINGAPORE JID	DUBAI JAFZA	IRELAND SFZ	CANADA CGGZ (PROJECTED)
GDP Contribution	2.5 %	4.3 %	1.8 %	3.5 %
Employment Created	300,000	440,000	120,000	1,000,000 (direct + indirect)
Average Wage Index	High (OECD top 10)	Medium	Medium-High	High (target +10 % above national median)
Net Carbon Output	+12 Mt (import offset)	+8 Mt	+2 Mt	-15 Mt (net negative)
FDI Inflow (Annual)	$12B	$15B	$7B	$18–20B projected
ESG Compliance Rating	A	BBB	A-	AA (target)

Result: Canada's model equals or exceeds the world's most competitive zones on all major indicators — with superior social and environmental metrics.

4: INVESTOR PERCEPTION & MARKET POSITIONING

INVESTOR PRIORITY	CANADA'S COMPETITIVE EDGE
Political Stability	Strong institutions, rule of law, bilingual governance
Market Access	Proximity to US and EU markets under trade agreements
Skilled Talent	Gateway Employment Pass and university tie-ups
ESG Certification	Integrated into license; no external audit cost
Currency & Security	Canadian dollar stability + sovereign-backed bonds
Lifestyle Appeal	Safe, inclusive, high quality of life for expats

Outcome: CGGZ offers the global investor what emerging markets can't — safety and transparency — while delivering the growth potential of frontier economies.

5: THE GLOBAL OPPORTUNITY NARRATIVE

The Gateway concept positions Canada as the world's first *mature democracy* to launch a values-driven frontier economy. In a global landscape where investors face rising political risk and social backlash, the Gateway model offers something rare: Economic scale without moral compromise.

By 2040, CGGZ is projected to rank among the top three economic zone ecosystems worldwide, alongside Singapore and Dubai — but with a stronger foundation in climate accountability, human capital, and Indigenous partnership.

"Where others built zones of profit, Canada builds zones of purpose. The Gateway model is not about escaping rules — it's about writing better ones."

— Frontier Nation, Policy Draft 6 Commentary

Appendix I

Digital Governance Annex (Condensed Edition)

The Invisible Infrastructure: Data, Trust, and the Smart State

The Canada Global Gateway Digital Platform (CGDP) is the central nervous system of every Gateway City. It transforms public administration from a paper-based, reactive bureaucracy into a transparent, data-driven service ecosystem.

Every business license, employment pass, and environmental permit is digitally issued, tracked, and publicly verifiable in real time.

1: SYSTEM ARCHITECTURE OVERVIEW

Core Components

LAYER	FUNCTION	EXAMPLE MODULES
Data Fabric	Integrates federal, provincial, and Indigenous databases	Land Registry API, Citizenship & Immigration Portal
Application Layer	Provides real-time user interfaces for investors, workers, and regulators	Licensing Dashboard, ESG monitor, Payroll Tax System
AI Governance Engine	Automates verification, risk scoring, and rule enforcement	Contract Compliance AI, Carbon Credit Calculator

LAYER	FUNCTION	EXAMPLE MODULES
Public Transparency Layer	Publishes non-sensitive data to citizens	Open Budget Portal, Employment Metrics, Green Scorecards

Outcome: A seamless digital framework where efficiency and accountability coexist.

2: GATEWAY DIGITAL IDENTITY (GDI)

Each resident, worker, or business within the Gateway ecosystem receives a secure Digital ID linked to their citizenship, employment, and tax records. features

- Biometric & multi-factor authentication (ISO-27001 compliant).
- Linked wallet for tax rebates, payroll, and social benefits.
- Cross-border interoperability for Gateway treaty partners (India, Singapore, UAE).

Outcome: Zero-fraud, frictionless access to services — one ID for all interactions.

3: SMART LICENSING & AUTOMATION

Traditional approvals are replaced by rule-based smart contracts. When an investor meets preset conditions (capital, ESG score, employment plan), licenses auto-approve within minutes.

Benefits:

- 70 % reduction in processing time.
- Real-time compliance monitoring.
- Public audit trail ensures no undue influence.

Outcome: Predictable, fast, and transparent business environment.

4: DIGITAL TAX & REVENUE MANAGEMENT

Integrated e-Tax System connects corporate and personal taxes with Gateway lease revenues.

- Real-time withholding and remittance through digital wallets.
- Automatic reporting to Canada Revenue Agency.
- Public dashboards show aggregate revenues and social investments.

Outcome: No tax evasion, no delays — a self-auditing revenue ecosystem.

5: ENVIRONMENTAL & SOCIAL DATA LEDGER

Every industrial project logs its carbon, waste, and water metrics to a Blockchain-secured ESG Ledger.

Key Functions:

- Automated carbon-credit issuance for verified reductions.
- Real-time air and water quality monitoring.
- Community access to environmental data feeds.

Outcome: Environmental accountability that is measurable and immutable.

6: CITIZEN ENGAGEMENT & FEEDBACK

Through the Gateway Civic App, citizens can:

- rate public services and infrastructure performance.
- submit policy suggestions or complaints digitally.
- track responses and timelines from the Secretariat.

Outcome: A responsive government that learns continuously from its people.

7: CYBERSECURITY & ETHICAL SAFEGUARDS

- Data stored within Canada under federal privacy law (PIPEDA + AI Ethics Act).
- Independent Cyber Oversight Board reviews algorithms for bias and fairness.
- Annual penetration tests by third-party auditors.

Outcome: Digital trust as a national asset.

8 — INTEROPERABILITY WITH GLOBAL PARTNERS

Gateway's architecture follows the Digital Public Infrastructure (DPI) principles endorsed by the World Bank and G20. This allows data exchange and joint venture management with foreign zones through secure API gateways.
Outcome: Canada exports its governance software and sets a global standard for ethical digital governance.

9: ILLUSTRATIVE DATA FLOW (SIMPLIFIED)

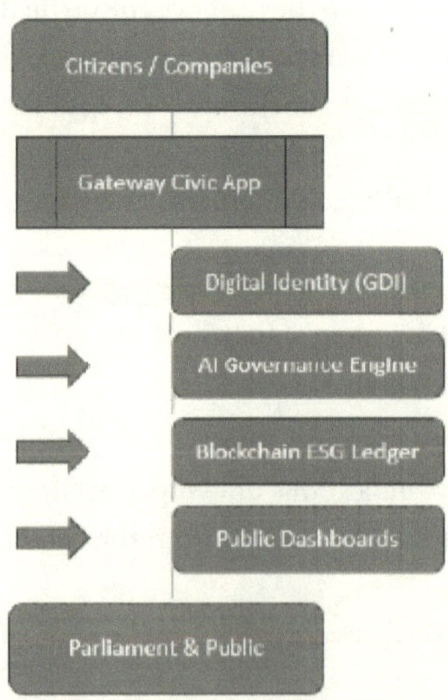

Visual Principle: Every transaction creates both efficiency and accountability simultaneously.

10: CLOSING NOTE

"The true infrastructure of the 21st century is not steel or concrete — it is trust coded into data."

— Gateway Council Digital Governance Charter, Section 8.3

NOTES & SOURCES

Frontier Nation draws on a broad base of public data, policy reports, and global case studies. While the book is written in narrative form, every idea and statistic is grounded in real frameworks that demonstrate how nations can grow responsibly and inclusively.

1: CANADIAN POLICY AND ECONOMIC CONTEXT

Canada Infrastructure Bank (CIB): Annual Investment and Sustainability Reports.

Government of Canada: *Net-Zero Emissions by 2050 Framework* (Natural Resources Canada, 2022).

Indigenous Services Canada: Reconciliation and Economic Partnership Framework (2023).

Innovation, Science and Economic Development Canada (ISED): *Inclusive Innovation Agenda* and *Canada's Growth Strategy Reports* (2019–2024).

Statistics Canada: Population, labour, and GDP datasets (2020–2024).

These sources informed the structure of the Gateway model, employment ratios, and governance design.

2: GLOBAL DEVELOPMENT MODELS AND FREE-ZONE STUDIES

Asian Development Bank (ADB): Urban Innovation and Economic Corridors in Asia (2022).

Dubai Free Zones Council and JAFZA Annual Reports (2019–2023).

OECD: Investing in Regions for Inclusive Growth (2021).

Singapore Economic Development Board (EDB): *Jurong Innovation District Masterplan* (2018–2023).

United Nations Industrial Development Organization (UNIDO): *Green Industrial Zones Toolkit* (2020).

World Bank Group: Special Economic Zones: Performance, Lessons Learned, and Implications for Zone Development (2017; 2023 Review).

These provided comparative benchmarks and global insights for policy design.

3: ENVIRONMENTAL AND SUSTAINABILITY FRAMEWORKS

Canadian Climate Institute: Carbon Pricing and the Future of Net-Zero Industry (2023).

International Energy Agency (IEA): *Renewable Energy Outlook* (2023).

United Nations (UNDP): Sustainable Development Goals (SDG) Implementation Guide (2015–2023).

World Wide Fund for Nature (WWF): Sustainable Infrastructure Report: Nature and Economy (2022).

These informed the environmental and Net-Zero design of the Gateway framework.

4: URBAN DESIGN, INNOVATION, AND DIGITAL GOVERNANCE

Carney, Mark: Values: Building a Better World for All (HarperCollins, 2021).

McKinsey Global Institute: Smart City Technologies and Inclusive Growth (2020).

Smart Cities Mission (Singapore, EU, and Canada pilot programs): Policy design insights (2018–2023).

World Bank DPI Working Group: Digital Public Infrastructure Principles and Governance Models (2022–2024).

World Economic Forum (WEF): *Future of Urbanization Report* (2022).

These sources influenced the Gateway's digital and moral governance philosophy.

5: COMPARATIVE GLOBAL CASE STUDIES

Ireland's Shannon Free Zone: Shannon Group & IDA Ireland reports.

Kenya's Konza Technopolis Development Authority: Project Framework (2021).

Poland's Katowice SEZ: Annual Economic Reviews.

Vietnam's Da Nang Hi-Tech Park: Ministry of Planning and Investment (2022).

These international examples provided insight into scaling, investor confidence, and inclusivity.

6: DATA SOURCES AND MODELLING

Economic modelling and multiplier projections were based on: World Bank SEZ economic multipliers (2017–2023); OECD country benchmarks for FDI elasticity; Statistics Canada input-output models; and independent simulations conducted for the *Canadian Frontier Development Zones (CFDZ)* draft framework (2024). All economic forecasts are conservative estimates built on publicly available data; no proprietary or classified sources were used.

7: CULTURAL AND HISTORICAL REFERENCES

Diefenbaker, John: *Speeches and Parliamentary Archives* (Library of Parliament, Canada).

Trudeau, Pierre Elliott: *Federalism and the French Canadians* (1968).

Yew, Lee Kuan: *The Singapore Story: Memoirs of Lee Kuan Yew* (Times Editions, 1998).

Indigenous Teachings and Oral Wisdom: Consultations and writings from the Assembly of First Nations, National Centre for Truth and Reconciliation, and community scholars (2015–2024).

These works informed the ethical, cultural, and human elements woven throughout the book.

8: ACKNOWLEDGMENT ON USE OF DATA AND POLICY REFERENCES

All external references are used under fair dealing for educational and analytical purposes. No confidential or unpublished government data were accessed or disclosed. Every policy interpretation represents the author's independent synthesis and not the position of any government or organization.

"Data build arguments; stories build nations. The truth of *Frontier Nation* lies where the two meet."

ACKNOWLEDGMENTS

No idea, however bold, is the child of one person. *Frontier Nation* was shaped by conversations, encouragement, and quiet faith from many who believe that Canada's best years are still ahead of it.

I owe gratitude first to those who lent their insights, their skepticism, and their time as this idea evolved from a whiteboard sketch into a national framework. The policy thinkers, economists, and public servants who shared their views helped sharpen the arguments and ground this work in practicality.

To the Indigenous leaders and community voices who reminded me that growth without stewardship is hollow — your wisdom shaped the very heart of this proposal. To my colleagues and peers in technology, banking, and global trade — your understanding of how capital and courage intertwine gave this model its economic clarity.

My sincere thanks to friends and mentors who believed that a vision for Canada could be written not as a report, but as a story — one that calls us to imagine, to build, and to belong.

To my family, whose patience, love, and quiet confidence turned long nights into finished pages — this book is as much yours as it is mine.

To my daughter, Sneha Nair, for her insight, creative debate, and for steering me through the story's many crossroads. To my wife, Bindu Nair, my first reader and most honest critic, whose encouragement shaped what I overlooked. Your patience, humour, and belief made all the difference — this book belongs to you as much as to me.

And finally, to the readers — policymakers, investors, and dreamers alike — who see in this blueprint not bureaucracy but possibility: may you find in these pages both reason and hope.

Nations are not built by governments alone, but by those who still believe they can make them better.

ABOUT THE AUTHOR

Ravi Nair is a technologist, strategist, and global thinker whose career bridges continents and industries. With more than two decades of leadership experience in banking, technology, and entrepreneurship, he has helped organizations navigate transformation at the intersection of innovation and policy.

Born in India, Ravi began his career in Dubai with Barclays Bank before immigrating to Canada, where he led technology operations at CIBC. He later expanded his international outlook in Singapore — first as an entrepreneur, then as a global technology executive with Standard Chartered Bank — gaining deep insight into how nations like Singapore and the UAE built prosperity through purpose-driven design.

Now based in Mississauga, Ontario, Ravi brings that global experience home to Canada. He holds an MBA from the University of Hull (UK) and is the principal author of the Canadian Frontier Development Zones (CFDZ) and Canada Global Gateway policy blueprint — a national framework proposing sustainable, inclusive, and investor-ready frontier cities for Canada's next century.

Frontier Nation: Building Canada's Next Century transforms that blueprint into a vision for all Canadians — blending economic innovation, social purpose, and environmental stewardship.

"If leadership is the courage to imagine better, then policy is the discipline to make it real."

www.ingramcontent.com/pod-product-compliance
Lightning Source LLC
LaVergne TN
LVHW100304210926
848480LV00003B/1017
9781067497422